THE
NICOTINE
CONSPIRACY

DEDICATION

In no book could the dedication be more
appropriate than this:

To Robin Hayley, my friend, colleague and successor.
And to his worldwide team of dedicated therapists
who, without exception, sacrificed highly paid and
successful careers to join our cause.

THE
NICOTINE
CONSPIRACY

ALLEN CARR

ARCTURUS

ARCTURUS

Arcturus Publishing Limited
26/27 Bickels Yard
151–153 Bermondsey Street
London SE1 3HA

Published in association with
foulsham
W. Foulsham & Co. Ltd,
The Publishing House, Bennetts Close, Cippenham,
Slough, Berkshire SL1 5AP, England

ISBN: 978-0-572-03441-2

This edition printed in 2008
Text copyright © 2008, Allen Carr's Easyway (International) Limited
Design copyright © 2008 Arcturus Publishing Limited

British Library Cataloguing-in-Publication Data: a catalogue
record for this book is available from the British Library

Printed in England by J. H Haynes & Co. Nr Yeovil, Somerset

CONTENTS

HITTING ONE'S HEAD AGAINST A BRICK WALL

Since Allen Carr's death in November 2006, his determination to rid the world of nicotine addiction lives on in the worldwide organization he created and the people he trained. Our tireless efforts at ALLEN CARR'S EASYWAY to comprehend and overcome the maze of red tape that stops our method being used by the NHS are testament to that fact.

The body that decides if the NHS will use a particular drug or treatment is the National Institute for Health and Clinical Excellence (NICE). We totally understand why there should be a system for deciding if public money is well spent. We applaud it. What we find so deeply frustrating is that this system makes it almost impossible for companies like ours to understand the rules which apply.

Moreover, even if you can fathom how the system works, you discover that you need to spend literally hundreds of thousands of pounds simply to comply with it. You might think, as we did, that with patient choice being such a central plank of government policy, anything that gives patients more choice might be welcomed. We were wrong and not only about this. Every step of our journey to make ALLEN CARR'S EASYWAY accessible to the public via the NHS has been met with brick wall after brick wall. You would think we were peddling poison rather than providing a safe method to cure nicotine addiction.

We have written repeatedly to people – high and low – in the NHS and Department of Health (DoH), inviting them to investigate our method. We always get the same response, which is that national policy on smoking needs to focus on 'accumulated evidence around efficacy and implementation'. To you and me, that means any method needs to be able to show that it works.

Fair enough, although we fail to understand, if this is the case, why the NHS endorses the use of nicotine-replacement therapy (NRT) and drugs such as Zyban and Champix when the evidence supporting these is vastly inferior to that supporting our method.

You might think, again as we did, that scientists are impartial and that the aim of science is nothing other than to get to the truth. Neither of these things are true, as we discovered.

This chapter in our learning curve began back in November 2004 when we applied to be formally assessed by NICE. We went on to present results from two independent studies, both conducted by scientists at the Institute of Environmental Health at the University of Vienna[1,2]. These established a success rate of more than 50 per cent for our method after one year. This far exceeds anything obtained by either NRT, Zyban or Champix. In addition to this, we have been operating for more than 20 years, have sold more than 10 million stop-smoking books and have a network of successful stop-smoking clinics in 40 countries. We were sure that with such great results, someone would take us seriously.

But in January 2005 we learned this was not to be. NICE assured us that the minutes of the meeting at which the decision was taken not even to evaluate our method would be made available to us. But when we requested them, we were refused. When we were finally forced to make a Freedom of Information request for a copy of the minutes, it was turned down on the basis of 'commercial interests', with no further explanation. However, NICE did confirm that the decision not to evaluate was taken by a panel which included representatives of the pharmaceutical industry.

When a new public health progamme on smoking cessation was being planned, this time looking at smoking cessation in the workplace (where the independent studies relating to our method had been set), we registered as a stakeholder in the process. This meant the studies that had been conducted on our method by respected scientists and published in peer review journals had at least to be acknowledged or a reason given.

That was in October 2005. Imagine our shock when, in February 2007, NICE produced its report on a mountain of evidence on various smoking-cessation methods specifically designed for the workplace. Ours, including one published in the *Internal Archives of Occupational Environmental Health* (2005)[1] and another in *Addictive Behaviors* (2006)[2], had again not been included. Tricia

Younger, the project leader of that report, responded to our dismay by simply saying that NICE felt our papers 'were promising but the programme development group felt there was insufficient evidence to support a recommendation on the EASYWAY method'.

According to these so-called experts, the science had not been thorough enough. Conducting scientific trials is new territory for a company that has thrived by word of mouth for more than twenty years. Our clinics offer a genuine money-back guarantee and our method has helped literally millions of people to stop smoking.

We are more than happy to comply with what is required but several years have now passed and more would be needed to meet these high standards that, incidentally, are not required elsewhere. When *Slimming World* was bidding to get its subscriptions paid for by the NHS via GP referral recently, it did so on the back of one study of 107 people.[3] Now around 12,000 vouchers for free 12-week programmes have been distributed via 30 primary care trusts. This is a far cry from the sort of evidence and processes that have been demanded from us and the *Slimming World* study would have cost a fraction of the costs which we are facing. The likely cost to our organization for undertaking the sort of Random Control Trial being demanded of us is around £500,000.

Moreover, we discovered that under its draft guidance NICE proposed to name ALLEN CARR'S EASYWAY as NOT recommended for coverage under the NHS. To isolate a single company takes NICE outside its already considerable remit. Its job is to evaluate drugs and treatments, not companies. But this is what happened when NICE finally issued its draft guidance on smoking cessation that would enable a whole range of new services to be approved on the NHS to help people stop smoking. This draft guidance specifically excluded ALLEN CARR'S EASYWAY.

Companies or individuals that have no evidence whatsoever of their ability to help smokers quit can apply to offer their services on the NHS but not ALLEN CARR'S EASYWAY. Such services include individual behavioural counselling, group behaviour therapy programmes, drugs or NRT, self-help materials and telephone counselling as well as quit-lines. All these things are provided by ALLEN CARR'S EASYWAY, with the exception, of course, of drugs or NRT.

We believe it is the fact that ALLEN CARR'S EASYWAY refuses to support NRT that has isolated us from the medical establishment.

We do not make this claim lightly and are all too aware that even bodies such as the Royal College of Physicians support NRT. This is not because nicotine is without harm, it says, but because it is less harmful than tobacco.

However, when we realized the extent to which we were being cold-shouldered we went back to basics and started looking at facts we could understand. One of the first things we learned is that there is a lot of money to be made from selling NRT, especially in the UK. The companies that make the gum, patches and inhalers operate a billion-dollar business that is growing fast. A fifth of revenues come from the UK, where non-

NHS, over-the-counter sales account for a spend of £1.66 per person per year. This compares with 69p in France, 18p in Germany, 22p in Italy and 19p in Spain.[4]

UK sales are growing at around 10 per cent a year while smoking is only going down by 0.4 per cent a year according to Action on Smoking (ASH). Not surprisingly NRT has proved unsuccessful in curing nicotine addiction and the reality is that the pharmaceutical industry is now competing with the tobacco industry to supply the nicotine-addicted market. People are spending £100 million[4] a year in UK chemists on NRT because they are addicted to nicotine. Moreover, they get their starter NRT packs courtesy of the taxpayer at NHS stop-smoking clinics.

Another revelation was the number of smoking-cessation experts who are in the pay of the companies that make NRT. These people conduct the studies that purport to show that NRT works and they all sing from the same song book to such an extent that a recent report from the Royal College of Physicians on smoking-cessation reads like a sales pitch for NRT.

Some of the scientists in the field have been quite upfront with us and said they couldn't support our method because we refuse to endorse the use of NRT. Others simply blanked us. Others still made such defamatory remarks about our methods that we have felt compelled to take legal action.

Our ongoing battle with the publicly funded charity, Action on Smoking (ASH), shows how the medical establishment sticks together. ASH made defamatory remarks about our success rate but, after intense pressure, has finally been forced to apologize unreservedly for making these statements in the national media and has agreed to pay our legal costs in full. When we contacted Professor Robert West from University College London's Department of Epidemiology and Public Health to see if we could help with his work with Cancer Research UK on finding new ways of helping smokers to quit, this prompted a letter in response saying, 'It would not be appropriate for Professor West, as someone who advises ASH on smoking cessation, to enter into correspondence on these matters.'

Another lesson was that the studies of NRT success rates classify an individual as a success if they say they have stopped smoking even though they are still taking nicotine via NRT. If there were alcohol patches which slowly released alcohol into the body, it would be little wonder that alcoholics would be better able to abstain from drinking than alcoholics with no alcohol being administered into their bodies. Likewise, nicotine addicts may find it easier to abstain from smoking initially when they are being given nicotine at the taxpayer's expense, but NRT cannot help them break their addiction. Indeed the idea that giving nicotine to a nicotine addict can possibly help them break their nicotine addiction is transparently absurd. Of course a majority of users revert to smoking quickly, continue to smoke *and* use NRT, or remain hooked on NRT long term.

Yet this is Government policy. Since we are talking about public money, it is important to realize how easily figures can fluctuate depending on what you are measuring. For example, NHS figures show that the cost per quitter was £194 in 2006/7. This is based on NHS Stop Smoking Services costing £36.4 million in 2006/7 and 188,162 people having said they had not smoked for four weeks (51 per cent success).[5]

But how many people do you know who have stopped smoking for four weeks and then started again? If you want the picture at 12 months, a meta-analysis published in the journal *Tobacco Control*, which is part of the BMJ Publishing Group, showed that only three in every ten people who have stopped at four weeks will still have stopped at 12 months.[6]

This has hugely important implications for the cost per quitter. The number of quitters falls to 56,448 and the cost per quitter at 12 months rises to £644.84. Add in advertising costs of £13.5 million that same year[7] and the cost per quitter at 12 months rises to £884. Add in the NHS spend of £50 million on NRT products in England and the cost per quitter at 12 months doubles to £1,768. Who knows what figures NICE used to calculate that NRT provides good value for money for the NHS.

The people who are actually responsible for local spending at Primary Care Trust (PCT) level also have their doubts. The *Health Service Journal* reported recently that Brent Teaching PCT had decided not to follow other PCTs which pay pharmacists £15 for each person they tried to get to stop smoking and a further £30 for everyone who was still not smoking at four weeks.[8] The author of that report, Daloni Carlisle, also raised the question of abuse. 'Stories abound,' she said, 'of unscrupulous advisers making up figures and of service users selling their free NHS patches.' The vast quantities of NRT for resale on eBay bear this out.

NICE's draft guidance also recommends Pfizer's Champix. The cost of a full course of Champix is £327.60. ASH claims that its success rate after one year is 22.5 per cent: this means that if ten smokers take it, the cost is £3,276 and just over two people will have stopped smoking after one year. The cost per quitter after a year comes out at £1,638, which is so similar to the costs of NRT one wonders if Pfizer's pricing policy wasn't based on the NRT figures.

The cost of a session at an ALLEN CARR EASYWAY clinic is £220, with two free back-up sessions for the minority who require them. If the smoker does not quit for at least three months, they can reclaim the fee in full.

ALLEN CARR'S EASYWAY deplores treating nicotine addiction with nicotine as that clearly cannot help break the addiction. In fact it simply prolongs it. We believe that many people in the medical establishment and the Government are aware of this but still promote NRT on the basis that it's not as bad for one's health as smoking. If that is the rationale, then policymakers should at least be honest with smokers and admit that NRT will not help them get free but is simply a damage limitation exercise. At our clinics we regularly get addicts who have stopped smoking but are still addicted years later to nicotine via NRT. ALLEN CARR'S EASYWAY has been so successful because it eliminates the need and desire for nicotine. Our method involves no drugs and is completely risk-free with no side-effects. The worst that can happen to a smoker attending one of our clinics is that they fail to quit, in which case their fee is refunded in full.

Nicotine carries its own risks. Its role in making cancers more aggressive, for example, is now so established that the mechanisms by which it encourages tumour growth are being investigated by researchers looking for new anti-cancer drugs. These risks are well documented. The *Journal of Health Psychology*, for example, outlines many of them, particularly those relating to the foetus, and concludes, 'The ultimate goal must be total cessation of smoking and nicotine intake in any form. NRT simply substitutes one form of nicotine for another but is neither safe nor as effective as other cessation aids.'[9]

The risks of nicotine are downplayed by the medical establishment because they are not as bad as those from smoking. We agree but believe that the price of remaining a slave to nicotine is being ignored and that the public should be allowed to decide these things for itself. Indeed, ALLEN CARR'S EASYWAY believes that the pharmaceutical industry is conspiring to use its incredible wealth, power and influence over governments, the medical establishment and the media to secure public policies which prolong nicotine addiction at the expense of the taxpayer and, of course, addicts themselves.

Support for this thinking comes from The *Journal of Health Psychology* when it says, 'Originally, the tobacco industry opposed the makers of NRT, but now both industrial enterprises seem to be finding common ground as tobacco and NRT have begun reinforcing each other and keeping the addiction to nicotine alive.'[9]

Robin Hayley, London 2008

REFERENCES

1 Hutter, H.P., Moshammer, H., Neuberger, M., 'Smoking cessation at the workplace: one year success of short seminars', *Internal Archives of Occupational Environmental Health* (2005)

2 Moshammer, H., Neuberger, M., 'Long-term success of short smoking-cessation seminars supported by occupational health care', *Addictive Behaviors* (2006)

3 Lavin, J.H. et al., 'Feasibility and benefits of implementing a slimming referral service in primary care using a commercial weight management partner', *Public Health*, Vol. 120, Issue 9, September 2006, pp. 872–8.

4 Nicholas Hall's DB6 2007 database (using an exchange rate of £1 to $2)

5 Statistics on NHS Stop Smoking Services in England, April 2006 to December 2006 (Q3 report)

6 Etter, J-F., Stapleton, J.A., 'Nicotine replacement therapy for long-term smoking cessation: a meta-analysis', *Tobacco Control 2006*: 15; 280–5

7 'Cuts hit smoking cessation efforts', *Health Service Journal*, May 9, 2007

8 'Will next month's ban fire up PCT stop-smoking services?', *Health Service Journal*, June 14, 2007

9 Ginzel, K.H. et al., 'Nicotine for the fetus, the infant and the adolescent', *Journal of Health Psychology*, 2007: 12; 215

PART 1

DEVASTATION

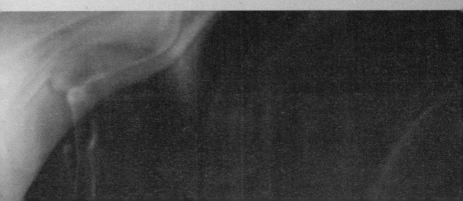

CHAPTER 1

THE GREATEST SCANDAL NEVER EXPOSED

You may have noticed that practically every week the media announce the discovery of a *possible* new 'wonder drug' or exciting new development, which might, just might, lead to the cure of a certain disease. Often, most people have never heard of the disease, let alone the requirement for a cure. In fact, recently the pharmaceutical industry has been openly accused of 'inventing' diseases for which drug companies have apparently discovered a cure. This 'wonder drug' culture helps to reinforce the belief that modern medicine is constantly producing miracle cures. Usually the announcement of a cure comes couched in cautionary terms such as:

'So far experiments have been carried out on mice and the results have proved encouraging. In five years, it is hoped that either a cure or treatment can be developed to alleviate the effects of the disease in humans.'

Millions of people suffer pain from arthritis, headaches, backaches and so on. Oh, how their hopes must be raised when they hear the announcement, only to be dashed when they've never heard of the disease. But just think how much more frustrating it would be if you actually suffered from that disease. Your lottery number comes up but you now have to wait five years, not necessarily to prove that the treatment will actually cure or relieve your condition, but to assess any potentially debilitating side-effects. The fact that the disease might have killed you in the meantime seems to have little bearing on the situation.

I can't remember how long ago these regular announcements started, but it seems to me it was after scientists began finding functions for our various genes, after James Watson and Francis Crick discovered the structure of DNA in 1953. Before biotechnology gave rise to such optimism, the medical profession had been trying to persuade us that our medical problems were mainly the result of our lifestyle: we smoked and drank too much, exercised too little and ate too much, particularly too much of the wrong foods.

I couldn't contradict the logic of these arguments. They were so obvious I couldn't understand why I'd ignored them for so many years. And when I finally saw the light and adopted them, no way could I refute that the vast improvement in my health was due entirely to those simple changes. But now it would appear that health has little to do with our lifestyle. Ignore the fact, if you can, that half the planet is dying from obesity and watches the other half die of starvation or polluted water. We are now being told our real problems lie with the incredibly sophisticated intelligence that created us. It makes not the slightest difference whether you believe that intelligence to be the God you worship or a process of Darwinian selection, apparently that intelligence blew it.

Bear in mind that process created us and not vice versa, and that the human body is a million times more sophisticated than the most complicated spaceship or computer mankind has been able to create. Also, bear in mind that although wild animals might suffer from starvation or being underweight, they are never overweight. Obviously, elephants will appear overweight compared to a stick insect; this is due to the needs of the particular species. Whatever the life form, each member is roughly the same shape and size, except with humans. Every day you can witness a human stick insect seated next to a human hippopotamus, but you will never see this with wild animals. This is because the recent and ever-changing so-called intelligence of mankind dominates our eating habits, whereas the habits of wild animals are based on three billion years of trial and error.

I find it somewhat ironic that so many research doctors explain their failure to find the solution to a problem – with the words:

'We need more research.'

Yet, at the same time:

IGNORE THREE BILLION YEARS OF RESEARCH

Similarly, the only person who has ever disputed my point about wild animals was a woman who wrote to me explaining how unhealthy her pet rabbits were. She then went into a lengthy discussion of their health problems and asked what I would advise. This was an intelligent lady, and I mention the point only to emphasize both the difficulty and necessity of keeping an open mind. The eating habits of pets and other domesticated animals are not dominated by Mother Nature but by so-called intelligent mankind.

The bulk of reliable medical knowledge has appeared only in the last two hundred years. Thalidomide and similar disasters are still fresh in my memory. There have even been instances where doctors have deliberately distorted the information on which their research was based.

Please ponder this question: *'How many medical announcements can you remember actually resulting in a proven and genuine benefit to the human race?'* If your memory is the same as mine, and with the exception of anti-infective drugs that can stem killer plagues, the answer will probably be: **NONE**.

Imagine that an immediate, genuine and inexpensive cure for cancer or AIDS was discovered. How long do you think it would take to broadcast the news around the world? Years? Months? Weeks? No. It would more likely be hours.

Further, assume that the cure involved no drugs, no surgery and no experiments on animals, needed no scientific studies or trials on human beings and had no side-effects whatsoever. How long do you think it would be before the disease was eradicated from the world? Surely, it would be a matter of weeks.

If the world's leading medical experts were aware of the doctor's claim but, for whatever reason, hadn't bothered to check it out and, more than twenty years after the discovery, were still advocating treatments that actually made the disease worse, would this not be a scandal on a gigantic scale?

Furthermore, assume that the world's media and politicians were also aware of the claims and not only chose to ignore them but actually encouraged the medical profession to continue with its traditional, ineffective methods. Wouldn't that be the biggest scandal of all time?

You are probably thinking that such a scenario couldn't happen in this enlightened day and age. If so, you'd be wrong. More than twenty years ago, I discovered an immediate, genuine and inexpensive cure for the number one killer disease in Western society. Amazingly, this good news hasn't been announced on a single TV or radio programme, or in any newspaper.

**I'M CONFIDENT THAT THIS IS THE
GREATEST SCANDAL IN THE HISTORY OF
MANKIND AND I INTEND TO EXPOSE IT**

TODAY!

CHAPTER 2

THE OBJECTIVES OF THIS BOOK

This book has three main objectives:

1 To establish Easyway as the only sensible way for any smoker to quit.

2 To establish that it is the policies of governments, the established medical profession and the media that make it difficult – if not impossible – for smokers to quit their nicotine addiction.

3 To eradicate this scandal as soon as possible. <u>Having achieved objects 1 and 2, to persuade 'the Big 3' to adopt Easyway universally.</u>

From the outset, I ask you to keep an open mind. From birth, we are all subjected to massive daily brainwashing, which distorts our true perspective of the world. Allow me to use Galileo as an example, particularly as my problem is similar to his. He was brave enough to contradict the unanimous opinion of the accepted authority of the day, namely the established Church, by suggesting that the earth moved around the sun and not vice versa. In fact, he was imprisoned for his effrontery and it took the Church more than 400 years to admit he was right. It wasn't until 1979 that Pope John Paul II admitted the Church's error and praised Galileo as a scientist.

Poor Galileo had his work cut out. He not only contradicted the experts, but everyone on the planet can clearly see that the sun rises in the East and sets in the West.

In fact it doesn't!
It only seems that way because of the perspective from which we view it.

Apart from Galileo, I don't suppose it made much difference to the daily lives of people in those days.

However, the myths and illusions I intend to expose have a disastrous effect on our lives and it is absolutely essential that you distinguish brainwashing, myth and illusion from fact. You can only do this if you start with your mind as a clean sheet. Ignore anything you have been told previously about the subject, no matter how often you have heard it repeated by people whose opinions you respect, or how expert you believe those people to be.

I will be presenting you with statements as established facts on both sides of the case and you will be the sole judge as to the truth. You might initially find some of the facts I present so outrageous that you conclude this is either a work of fiction or the author has escaped from a mental institution. Neither is the case. In fact, I'm widely accepted as the world's leading expert on this disease, even by the medical profession, the media and politicians. However, you must be sceptical about me. If I can establish the statement as a fact at the time, I will do so and it will be up to you whether you accept it. Otherwise, I will prove the point in due course. All I ask is that, if at any time you are tempted to cast this book into the rubbish bin, please **DON'T!** Unfortunately, what is basically a very simple concept has been made unnecessarily complex by brainwashing, myths and illusions and it is not always possible to remove them in the sequence we need to follow.

It is also essential to stick rigidly to the sequence in which the book has been written. You can always refer back to refresh, but to jump forward would create confusion. The key at this stage is to open your mind to the fact that no matter how outrageous any statement may appear – and I don't expect you to accept it at the time – I will prove it in due course.

I have one final warning before we proceed. You may have already formed the impression that I am an arrogant, big-headed so-and-so. If so, I apologize. However, I have important information to reveal and regret I cannot afford the luxury of false modesty. So please just accept that I'm presenting the facts in the most honest way I can and try not to let my manner divert your attention from that important information.

At our stop smoking clinics, in order to make a particular point, I'm in the habit of drawing a smoker's attention to a particular pattern of behaviour. At times in this book I have forgotten that I'm not only addressing smokers but ex-smokers and people who have never smoked, and have found myself making statements like: **'Take six deep, consecutive inhalations now!'** Unless you are a smoker, please ignore any such instruction. It would indeed be a tragedy if, in my desire to rid the world of nicotine addiction, I were unwittingly to increase the number of smokers.

We can now turn to the disease I am referring to. Have you heard about:

DEVASTATION?

CHAPTER 3

DEVASTATION

DEVASTATION is an extract from a plant indigenous to South America, of the same family as deadly nightshade (*Solanaceae*). It is the most addictive drug known to mankind. More than 60 per cent of adults become hooked. It is a powerful poison and is used commercially as an insecticide. It gradually breaks down the immune system, causes breathlessness and lethargy and, according to the latest medical statistics, kills one in two of those who are unfortunate enough to become addicted to it. It tastes foul and systematically destroys the nervous system, causing a feeling of insecurity and lack of confidence. It currently costs the average UK addict around £100,000 over a lifetime. What does it do for them?

ABSOLUTELY NOTHING!

Could I persuade you to try it? Of course not. Who would be that stupid?

If you were addicted to it and you knew of an easy, immediate, permanent and inexpensive cure, wouldn't you take advantage of it without hesitation? If your answer is no, then you've no need to doubt my sanity. On the contrary, start doubting your own. Can you believe that more than 99 per cent of the population of Western society has experimented with this drug and at one time more than 90 per cent of adult males were actually addicted to it?

The more discerning reader will already have deduced that Devastation is the drug we know as nicotine, or to put it another way: being a smoker. But let's be honest, what smoker, ex-smoker or lifelong non-smoker would see the *smoking habit* in that light? Incidentally, I've styled such phrases as *smoking habit, giving up smoking, happy smoker* etc., in italics because they are common illusions. As I will explain shortly, smoking isn't a *habit* but nothing more or less than *addiction* to nicotine.

If you find that concept difficult to accept, ponder the question:

Do cocaine sniffers do it because they enjoy sniffing or because they are addicted to coke?

If I were writing this book 150 years ago, I would be asking you:

Do people sniff snuff because they enjoy sniffing, or because they are addicted to nicotine?

Snuff-taking was a common form of nicotine addiction before cigarettes. It too was a filthy, disgusting *habit* and, just as silver and gold cigarette cases and lighters were once fashionable, trappings such as silver snuff boxes were used to make it appear sociable and acceptable. Incidentally, if you have visions of switching to a pipe or an occasional cigar, forget it. References to cigarettes include anything containing nicotine. I emphasize this is good news not bad!

NICOTINE ADDICTION IS THE MOST INGENIOUS CONFIDENCE TRICK THAT MOTHER NATURE AND MANKIND HAVE COMBINED TO PLAY!

A confidence trick is an illegal operation by which an otherwise honest person is swindled. An example will help. A couple save all their lives for the perfect retirement home. After much searching they find exactly that: the location, the house and the garden are all better than they'd hoped for. The sellers even agree to a reduction in the purchase price. The buyers willingly put down a large deposit, which represents the down payment.

The operation starts off smoothly, but then snags begin to creep in. Eventually, the couple become suspicious and decide to drop out but they can't get their money back. It turns out that the agent has sold to, and taken deposits from, dozens of other buyers. But aren't such deposits refundable? They are if the agent is honest, but this agent happens to be a con artist and takes off with their money.

Perhaps the couple could have been described as

happy house buyers until they discovered the whole operation was a mere confidence trick. If they'd had the full facts at the beginning, no way would they have been buyers, let alone *'happy buyers'!*

Now, please re-read my definition of Devastation at the beginning of the chapter, reproduced here for your convenience:

DEVASTATION is an extract from a plant indigenous to South America, of the same family as deadly nightshade (*Solanaceae*). It is the most addictive drug known to mankind. More than 60 per cent of adults become hooked. It is a powerful poison and is used commercially as an insecticide. It gradually breaks down the immune system, causes breathlessness and lethargy and, according to latest medical statistics, kills one in two of those who are unfortunate enough to become addicted to it. It tastes foul and systematically destroys the nervous system, causing a feeling of insecurity and a lack of confidence. It currently costs the average UK addict around £100,000 over a lifetime.

You can check out all the facts for yourself. But is that how we see the somewhat dangerous, expensive and filthy pastime of being a smoker? Let me make it clear. The optimist sees the bottle as half full, the pessimist sees it as half empty. We need to see, and ensure that our children see, the reality:

THE TOBACCO BOTTLE IS FULL

AND IT'S FULL OF POISON!

In fact, the only statement with which you could possibly disagree is that smoking does absolutely nothing for the smoker.

While people retain the distorted view that smoking is a pleasure and a crutch, smoking will continue to attract an endless supply of new recruits.

I intend to prove to you that smoking provides no benefits or advantages whatsoever, that whether they realize it or not every smoker wants to quit and that my method – which I call Easyway for reasons that will become obvious – will enable any smoker to do so easily, immediately and permanently. We are already agreed that no one apprised of the full facts would either continue to smoke or start smoking. In the meantime, start seeing smokers as simply addicted to **Devastation.**

If you have difficulty in accepting the mere idea of it being easy to quit, then ask around. You'll find dozens of smokers have achieved it. The problem is they don't understand themselves exactly why it was easy, and may give you advice that has the opposite effect. With Easyway, precise instructions are given that make it easy for every smoker to quit.

The phrase *'It's just a habit!'* is probably the most common and damaging of all the illusions. *'I'm trying to give up smoking'* is almost as common and equally damaging. It implies that the would-be ex-smoker is making a genuine sacrifice. The beautiful truth is that there is absolutely nothing to *give up*.

Let's just take a brief glance at how society has generally regarded smoking in recent years.

Before 1954, when Professor Richard Doll dropped his bombshell about the connection between lung cancer and cigarette smoking, it was generally regarded as an enjoyable and sociable pastime. In fact, male non-smokers tended to be treated with suspicion. I'm sure most people regarded the announcement as a mortal blow to the *habit*. Amazingly, at the age of 22 – already a chain smoker with a permanent smoker's cough – it didn't change my attitude one iota.

The lung cancer scare was followed at regular intervals by other health scares: passive smoking, damage to foetuses, among others. Society's general attitude to smoking was gradually changing, and it went from being a pleasant, sociable pastime to a decidedly antisocial nuisance. Then the bans came in on advertising and public transport, as well as in public buildings, cinemas and theatres, offices, factories, pubs and restaurants. Teachers were training pupils to emotionally blackmail their parents into *giving up*.

It seemed to me that the tobacco industry was in a similar position to Hitler during the latter stages of the Second World War; in retreat on all fronts and surrounded by three powerful armies – the Americans, the Russians and the British, who had massive additional support from the Commonwealth and many other countries. He was already fighting a lost cause.

What chance did the tobacco industry have when in addition to the above it was opposed by three powerful institutions, all supposedly committed to combating nicotine addiction?

1 GOVERNMENTS

2 THE ESTABLISHED MEDICAL PROFESSION

3 THE MEDIA

Let's refer to them as **'the Big 3'**.

Remember that Professor Doll delivered his blow more than half a century ago and in spite of bans on advertising, national and world No Smoking Days, and the massive initiatives of **'the Big 3'**, he tobacco industry appears to be thriving.

You've no doubt heard the expression: *There are lies, damn lies and statistics.* I was a chartered accountant. Statistics were one of the tools of my trade. That's one of the reasons I hated being an accountant. Have you noticed after each Government initiative they quote statistics to justify its success?

Now consider this **FACT:** the World Health Organization (WHO) has indicated that current annual deaths worldwide from smoking exceed five million and that by 2020 that figure will have risen to ten million.

It goes as far as to say that tobacco is the second major cause of death in the world, is currently responsible for the death of one in ten adults worldwide and that half the people who smoke today – that is about 650 million people – will eventually be killed by tobacco.

Does that sound as if 'the Big 3' are in control of the problem?

THE TRUTH IS THAT WE'VE FAILED EVEN TO PREVENT OUR CHILDREN AND GRANDCHILDREN FROM FALLING INTO THE TRAP. THOSE SAME YOUNGSTERS, WHO WERE DESPERATELY TRYING TO PERSUADE THEIR PARENTS TO QUIT ARE NOW PUFFING AWAY AS IF SMOKING NEVER WENT OUT OF FASHION!

PLEASE HELP ME TO REMOVE THIS EVIL

Smoking killed my father in his mid-fifties and my sister in her mid-forties. Once the brainwashing, illusions and cobwebs have been removed, I believe the word Devastation is an apt description of the drug nicotine. However, the word has another connotation. Allow me to refer briefly to the way smoking devastated my life.

CHAPTER 4

THE WAY SMOKING DEVASTATED MY LIFE

Picture a happy, extremely fit, sports-mad 15-year-old. Jump a third of a century and try to visualize a miserable, pathetic, irritable, lethargic, obese, lacklustre old man, chain smoking sixty to a hundred cigarettes a day. Each morning I would struggle to get out of bed. Before I'd even put a stitch of clothing on, there would be a cigarette dangling from my lips.

I had a permanent smoker's cough, regular bouts of asthma and bronchitis and, occasionally, made my nose bleed with the pressure of coughing. Most smokers block their minds to cancer scares in the belief that they will quit before it happens. I'd long gone past that stage. I didn't think I'd live long enough to contract lung cancer. The vein running down the centre of the forehead is rather prominent on some people. I could feel the pain caused by the pressure that my coughing was exerting on that vein. I'd heard opera singers were vulnerable to brain haemorrhages because of the pressure caused when reaching the high notes. In fact, I believe the great Caruso died of one.

Any moment, I was expecting an explosion in my

head and for blood to start pouring out of my mouth, ears and eyes. If you are a smoker, you are probably thinking you too would have quit had you got to that stage. But I didn't quit because of that. On the contrary, at that stage I was prepared to die.

Be you non-smoker or smoker, you will also probably be thinking I was incredibly stupid not to stop at that stage. If so, please remember the medical profession now claims that smoking kills one smoker in two. Both Einstein and Freud died from it. Furthermore, if you've ever had to witness a close friend or relative dying of lung cancer, emphysema, asthma or bronchitis, particularly if they have also had limbs removed because of smoking, you will know they don't die peacefully in their sleep. Most go through months, or even years, of agony and misery. Do you think it helps smokers to believe they are stupid enough actually to choose that death, or that they are lacking in the willpower necessary to *give up*?

Another common myth about smoking is that heavy smokers enjoy smoking most. It sounds logical, why else would they smoke so much? I loathed smoking both before I was hooked and afterwards. Like most youngsters, I can also remember hating those first experimental cigarettes and how hard I had to work in order to inhale without feeling sick or having a coughing fit.

I made several serious attempts to quit. After each failure, the loathing intensified. The penultimate attempt was two years before discovering Easyway. I was fully aware that if I didn't succeed, I'd soon be dead.

Ex-smokers, who had *given up* by using willpower, told me it was difficult to begin with but as time went by it got easier, rather like mourning a close relative or friend and that, in time, the cravings become so few and far between they cease to be a problem. I went through week after week of abject misery. Not only did it not ease up, it just got worse and worse and after six months of purgatory I caved in.

Perhaps six months doesn't sound very long when your life depends on it. But, just as chronic alcoholics believe they are different from normal drinkers, I believed I was a chronic 'smokaholic' and could never be free. I'd been trying to solve a simple problem, one that most ten-year-olds would find a piece of cake. But my brain just wouldn't function. I lit a cigarette and hey presto – problem solved! Positive proof that smoking helps concentration. I had a clear choice: either to spend the rest of my life a simpleton or start smoking again. With the distorted knowledge I had about smoking at that time, there could be only one answer.

Later, I often pondered whether I might have succeeded if I'd managed to survive another week, month or whatever. However, I'm now certain that whilst I retained a distorted view about smoking, I would have had to continue using willpower until it ran out.

I was going through very mixed emotions when I finally capitulated and lit that cigarette. The first was utter relief at no longer having to resist temptation. That frustration disappeared as quickly as my concentration returned. At the same time, I was in tears because I knew I'd let my wife, Joyce, down again and that, my best shot having failed, I was doomed to remain a smoker for life and didn't expect to reach the age of 50.

Like all smokers who try to quit and fail, I felt very stupid. But was it such a stupid decision? Surely the shorter, more enjoyable life of the *happy smoker* is preferable to the longer, more miserable life of the ex-smoker? One of the major illusions I shall disprove is that:

THERE IS NO SUCH THING AS A HAPPY SMOKER!

In any event, I made up my mind to accept my fate and decided I would never even attempt to *give up* again. However, a couple of years later certain things happened in close proximity and I decided to give it one final try. I'm very happy to now be able to pass on to Part 2:

EXALTATION

EXALTATION

CHAPTER 5

EXALTATION

My final attempt started on the morning of 15 July 1983. I'd taken the precaution of taking a few days off work so as not to put undue pressure on myself. It started off like any previous attempt to quit that involved the use of willpower. I was in no physical pain but had the usual feeling of foreboding, anticipating at least six months of misery before I had any hope of succeeding.

Again, to avoid putting pressure on myself I hadn't told anyone other than my wife Joyce that I was making another attempt to *give up*. But, unbeknown to me, she had mentioned it to my eldest son John and shortly after midday he called in to give me some support. I hope I didn't betray my true feelings, since the last thing I needed was to listen to someone mouthing the usual platitudes. I just wanted to be left alone to wallow in my misery.

To make matters worse, John had brought with him one of those Do-It-Yourself medical guides, containing a chapter on smoking which he thought might be useful to me. Out of politeness, I didn't tell him I already knew that smoking was killing me. Instead

I thanked him and dutifully read the chapter. It was medical gobbledygook, containing phrases like: *'A drug which increases the likelihood of its own self-administration is known by behavioural psychologists as a reinforcer of drug-taking behaviour.'*

I had some cigarettes left over from the previous day and decided that when I'd finished smoking those, that would be it. After John left, I set about polishing them off. John had left the book and I'm not sure why but I started to read the chapter again and again. To begin with, it was still gobbledygook. But then something very strange began to happen. Have you ever seen one of these pictures that consists of a complicated pattern and if you stare at the pattern for long enough and allow your eyes to go out of focus, suddenly a picture of a horse, or whatever, appears as if by magic in 3D? Blink your eyes and it disappears. As I re-read the gobbledygook, a startling fact began to emerge.

To me, being a smoker was a complete paradox. I knew it was killing me and costing a fortune. I knew I could enjoy life and cope with stress before I fell into the trap. I knew I was both reasonably intelligent and strong-willed. Yet, there I was, loathing myself for being a smoker and at the same time completely dependent and unable to *give up*.

The only possible explanations that made sense were:

1 There was some magic in smoking that did help me to concentrate and relax.

2 There was some weakness in my genetic make-up, such as an addictive personality.

3 I wasn't as strong-willed as I thought I was.

In an instant, the paradox, the mysteries, the mists, the doubts and the confusion all evaporated and no amount of blinking could make them return. The gist of the article was that when nicotine leaves your body it creates an empty, insecure feeling. When you light up, the first few puffs replace the nicotine and the empty, insecure feeling immediately disappears; and you do actually feel more relaxed or less stressed than you did a moment before.

Imagine devoting your entire lifetime to studying Egyptian hieroglyphics, absolutely obsessed with the subject, yet unable to find the key to break the code. Then imagine discovering the clue that made everything so simple and clear that you spend the rest of your life wondering why it hadn't always been so obvious. I realized I'd discovered the solution to the most ingenious confidence trick that Mother Nature and mankind together have been able to play.

For years I believed it was Abraham Lincoln who said:

'You can fool all of the people some of the time and some of the people all of the time, but you can't fool all of the people all of the time!'

I'm now told that credit for the statement should go to P.T. Barnum, the famous American circus impresario.

I'm inclined to agree, since one would expect the world of the circus to be more closely associated with illusion than 'Honest Abe'. On second thoughts many, including myself, believe the worlds of circus and politics are a pretty close thing as far as spin and illusion are concerned.

In any event, whether it was Lincoln or Barnum, it just goes to prove how easily people can be fooled. I doubt whether the Barnum devotee would have made the contradiction unless he knew he was correct.

UNTIL MY DISCOVERY ON 15 JULY 1983, I BELIEVE THE NICOTINE TRAP HAD DONE JUST THAT:

FOOLED EVERYBODY!

Surely that cannot be true. Millions of people have never fallen into the trap. That is so, but millions of mice have never fallen into a mousetrap and that doesn't mean they understand how it works.

Now try to imagine the utter joy of the Count of Monte Cristo, never expecting to escape from that dungeon, to suddenly find himself a free man. Perhaps this will help you to understand the absolute exaltation I felt at that moment and why I've never lost that feeling.

I knew immediately that I was already a non-smoker and would never have the slightest need or desire to smoke again. I went overnight from chain smoking to zero, without suffering any withdrawal pangs, physical or mental, or suffering any period of depression. It took no willpower whatsoever. I immediately enjoyed social occasions more and felt better equipped to handle stress. In fact, I thoroughly enjoyed the whole process, actually lost weight, and have never had the slightest temptation to smoke since!

For obvious reasons, I refer to my method as Easyway, and it didn't take me long to realize that it would work just as effectively for all smokers.

I must emphasize that be you smoker, ex-smoker or non-smoker, no way do I expect you to understand the clarity with which I saw the nicotine trap at that time or the dramatic effect it had on me. Bear in mind I'd already spent years pondering the mysteries of the nicotine trap. Also bear in mind that I will prove to you that our *habit* of smoking is nothing more or less than addiction to the drug I described as Devastation at the beginning of chapter 3.

Allow me to explain more about:

THE NICOTINE TRAP

CHAPTER 6

THE NICOTINE TRAP

Contrary to popular belief, nicotine is not the brown chemical that tends to stain smokers' fingers and teeth. It's a colourless, oily compound and is the drug contained in tobacco that addicts the smoker. It is the fastest addictive drug known to mankind and it can take just one cigarette to become hooked.

Every puff on a cigarette delivers, via the lungs to the brain, a small dose of nicotine that acts more rapidly than the dose of heroin the addict injects into his veins.

If there are 20 puffs in a cigarette, you receive 20 doses of the drug with just one cigarette.

Nicotine is a quick-acting drug and levels in the bloodstream fall quickly to about half within two hours of smoking a cigarette. This explains why most smokers average about 20 per day.

Nicotine is also a powerful poison and is used commercially as an insecticide. If you were to inject the nicotine content of just one cigarette directly into a vein, it would kill you.

When nicotine leaves the body, the smoker begins to suffer withdrawal pangs. At this stage I need to dispel two common illusions. The first is that withdrawal pangs are the terrible trauma smokers suffer when they try to *give up*. This is mainly mental – the same feeling that sends smokers out in the middle of the night searching for an all-night garage. Since the smoker often hasn't actually completely run out at this stage, that panic feeling can only be caused by a mental process. In fact, smokers suffer nicotine withdrawal pangs throughout their smoking lives and that is the only reason they light the next cigarette.

The second illusion is that withdrawal pangs from nicotine involve physical pain. There is physical withdrawal but, like hunger for food, it involves no pain.

As I will explain later, it is strictly incorrect to describe nicotine withdrawal pangs as: *'craving a cigarette'*. However, until we reach that explanation, for convenience I will use that expression.

In truth, one of the great ingenuities of the nicotine trap is that the withdrawal pangs are almost imperceptible so that smokers don't even realize they exist. They only know the feeling as:

'I WANT OR NEED A CIGARETTE!'

Undoubtedly the best news of all is that, although nicotine is the most powerful drug known to mankind in the speed it can addict you, you are never badly addicted and the actual withdrawal pangs get no worse when you extinguish the final cigarette. If you have experienced, as I did many times, the misery of trying to *give up* using a willpower method (any method other than Easyway), you will find this very difficult to believe, but don't lose faith. Easyway has gained its reputation precisely because it removes that misery.

The situation is further confused because the feeling caused by nicotine withdrawal is indistinguishable from the feeling caused by normal hunger and normal stress.

When the smoker lights up to satisfy the craving, the nicotine is replaced and the empty, insecure feeling is immediately relieved. The smoker does actually feel more relaxed, less nervous and better able to concentrate than a moment before. But what is the true position? The current cigarette has merely removed the empty, insecure feeling created by the first cigarette and perpetuated by every subsequent one.

This is why there is this continuous chain effect to being a smoker. Lobster has long been my favourite food. But I never reached the stage whereby I had to have twenty lobsters hanging around my neck, and I never got into a panic if lobster was not on the menu. Try to see the chain effect of smoking as it really is; each cigarette causing, rather than relieving, the empty, insecure feeling and automatically ensuring the need for the next.

I used to call myself a nicotine addict. It never occurred to me that I was actually addicted to a drug. It was just a colloquial expression. I also used to refer to myself as a golf addict. How do you distinguish them? Easy! I loved playing golf and wanted to play more and more. I loathed being dominated by that filthy 'weed' yet believed I couldn't live without it.

Another illusion is that smokers get some genuine 'hit', 'buzz' or 'high' when they light up. In fact they never do. In truth, the entire cycle is like wearing tight shoes just to get the pleasure of removing them occasionally. The only physical 'hit', 'buzz' or 'high' is actually dizziness, caused by starvation of oxygen to the brain. You can get exactly the same feeling if you spin around in a circle for ten seconds, which doesn't kill you, cost you a fortune or ruin your life – it simply makes you dizzy.

The tight-shoes analogy illustrates that although there are many pathetic aspects to being a smoker, undoubtedly the most pathetic of all is that the only 'pleasure' a smoker obtains when they breathe those filthy, cancerous fumes into their lungs is to get back to the same feeling of relaxation they enjoyed during the whole of their life as a non-smoker.

Perhaps you think that feeling of pleasure is not just illusion but real. After all, the smoker does feel more relaxed, confident and better able to concentrate when relieving the withdrawal pangs. However, cigarettes don't actually relieve them. On the contrary, each dose of nicotine creates the withdrawal pangs.

In fact, the true position is far worse than it might at first appear. As stated, nicotine is a powerful poison and one of our body's natural defences is to build tolerance of the poison. However, tolerance is a double-edged sword; it not only gives our body partial protection from the harmful effects of smoking, but it ceases to relieve the withdrawal pangs completely. The effect is that even whilst you are smoking a cigarette, you will never feel as relaxed as you did as a non-smoker. To describe smoking as relaxing is equivalent to describing the wearing of tight shoes as relaxing!

Let's quickly dispose of some more bad news. Some smokers are under the impression that if they don't inhale tobacco they won't get hooked. You might not be conscious of breathing but you obviously do it. In fact, in my opinion, the worst thing smokers inflict on non-smokers is not passive smoking but nicotine addiction itself. One reason that nicotine is the most addictive drug known to mankind is that you can be weaned on to it without actually smoking yourself.

But can the nicotine trap really be as simple as I have stated and, if so, why isn't it obvious? Don't underestimate the ingenuity of the trap. The main problem is that, like all drug addiction, it works back to front. It's when you aren't smoking that you suffer the empty, insecure feeling and the moment you light up that you seem to relieve it. Little wonder our brains are fooled into believing we get a genuine boost. I've already referred to the massive brainwashing to which we are subjected from birth. However, I believe the factor which makes the nicotine trap so potent is:

THE CLOSE ASSOCIATION BETWEEN CRAVING NICOTINE AND HUNGER

CHAPTER 7

THE CLOSE ASSOCIATION BETWEEN CRAVING NICOTINE AND HUNGER

We often claim that you can reap no more out of this life than the benefits of the seeds you sow, but is that strictly true? Most of us generally regard hunger as a terrible evil, which must be avoided. But is hunger such a terrible thing?

Let me make it absolutely clear that I distinguish between hunger and starvation. Starvation is one problem that most of the human race has managed to solve, even though the solution seems to have led to another killer: **OBESITY**! If your record is anything like mine, the longest you'll have gone without food was to miss the occasional meal. That can hardly be described as starvation. Yet, how often have you heard people say, *'I'm starving!'*, sometimes even before a meal is due?

If you were Mother Nature and had created this incredible variety of species, how would you ensure they didn't all starve? You'd need to arrange sufficient supplies of food and, in order to ensure the food was eaten you'd need to invent an ingenious device called hunger.

We tend to think that we eat because food tastes

good. This is not strictly true. It is not just coincidence that the French wish you '*bon appetit*' (good appetite) before a meal rather than 'good food', or that Asians eat rice as their staple diet, while Italians prefer pasta and the English potatoes. Nor is it coincidence that initially your mother's cooking is the best and eventually, if you are lucky, it becomes your partner's. I love the ritual of eating out, but if I really want to enjoy food there's no place like home.

If you're in the habit of eating good food – as opposed to junk – that genuinely satisfies your appetite and supplies your body with the energy and nutrients it requires to lead a healthy and active life, you will not feel hungry between meals. When your next meal is due, you can then enjoy the luxury of satisfying your hunger. Even if occasional meals are overdue, hunger involves no physical pain. OK, your stomach might be making its feelings known, but that isn't pain.

Similarly, if a smoker smokes 20 cigarettes a day, he or she might not be even aware of the craving until the next cigarette is due. The smoker can then light up and *enjoy* 20 cigarettes a day throughout their lifetime. Of course, the enjoyment is merely an illusion. Even so, the smoker will be successfully deluded since they believe each cigarette is satisfying rather than causing the aggravation. Little wonder that if a smoker's finances won't run to both food and cigarettes, cigarettes take preference every time.

Although, to the smoker, smoking appears to give the same sort of pleasure as eating, in reality the two are diametrically opposed for several reasons:

1 Food does taste good and the process of eating is a genuine pleasure; whereas trying to satisfy a craving for nicotine consists of inhaling foul, cancerous fumes into your lungs.

2 Food is essential to our survival and provides us with the energy and nutrients to live long, happy and healthy lives; whereas smoking consists of taking regular doses of poison that make us breathless, lethargic and unhealthy and just happens to be the number one cause of various killer diseases.

3 Far from creating the aggravation of hunger, food genuinely relieves it; whereas far from relieving the craving, the first cigarette creates it and each subsequent cigarette simply perpetuates it.

Once this became clear to me, the confusion I had suffered about smoking disappeared.

CHAPTER 8

ALL WAS REVEALED!

All was revealed to me on 15 July 1983. I told my wife Joyce:

'I'M GOING TO CURE THE WORLD OF SMOKING!'

In an instant I had been transformed from the most hopeless nicotine addict on the planet to the world's leading, and at that stage only, expert on nicotine addiction. Needless to say, Joyce didn't believe me and nor did any of my other friends or relatives.

I take this opportunity to put the record straight. Presumably because I was a chartered accountant, it has been assumed that my greedy eye recognized my discovery as an opportunity to exploit my fellow nicotine sufferers. It is true that I believed I could cure any smoker in ten minutes merely by explaining the true nature of the nicotine trap, as I have above. What I hadn't realized was that before I could get them to believe me, I first had to remove the myths, illusions and brainwashing they had been subjected to since birth.

I wrote to Edwina Currie, then the Junior Health Minister, who was portraying herself as a 'health champion' of the people. Now I do not think it was unreasonable to assume that a servant of the public, particularly a Minister of Health, would be just slightly interested in something that would save the lives of more than 100,000 UK citizens every year. I received this reply on 23 March 1987:

'Mrs Currie has asked me to thank you for sending her Allen Carr's book on smoking. It was a very kind thought and Mrs Currie is grateful to you – she hopes Mr Carr will continue to persuade further converts.'

The letter was signed by Mary Grafton, Private Secretary. I suppose it was too much to expect Edwina to answer the letter personally. Perhaps I was being unreasonable. No doubt she was right to focus on salmonella in eggs – after all, about five people had died of it and we have to get our priorities right.

However, you'd have thought a Junior Health Minister would have been just slightly interested in a simple and immediate cure for a disease that was killing more than 100,000 British citizens a year at the time. I admit I was very disappointed. Among others, I wrote to *The Times*, the British Medical Association (BMA), Action on Smoking and Health (ASH), the *Lancet*, Glasgow 2000 and the Director General of the BBC. There I was, eager to share my discovery with the rest of the world, and its attitude was: **Don't call me. I'll call you!**

I regret that the excitement of my discovery had

closed my mind to the realities of the world. However, it didn't take long to sink in. Why should anyone listen to me? I had no medical qualifications whatsoever and no credibility. I was left with only one option:

TO PROVE THAT EASYWAY IS NOT JUST BY FAR THE MOST EFFECTIVE METHOD TO QUIT SMOKING BUT THE ONLY METHOD THAT ALL SMOKERS SHOULD BE USING.

I have no need to continue to blow my own trumpet. After 23 years, I have the support of a worldwide network of dedicated therapists, all of whom managed to escape the nicotine trap with the help of Easyway and gave up worthwhile and lucrative professions because the merits of the method were obvious to them also. Easyway is widely accepted as the most effective quit-smoking method in the world. Our credibility is already established.

Bear in mind that in establishing that credibility we have not had access to the massive advertising budgets, Government and charitable support that our rivals have enjoyed and continue to enjoy. We have not been able to advertise Easyway. Initially, it was the work of one man and it has achieved its reputation by word of mouth for one reason and one reason alone:

BECAUSE IT WORKS!

You might also have heard that Easyway doesn't work for some people or is merely a philosophy or a series of tips. Not so! The beautiful truth is that any smoker can quit easily and painlessly. It's the other methods that make it difficult. Easyway consists of a set of instructions similar to those necessary to open the combination lock to a safe. Follow the instructions precisely and you cannot fail to escape.

WARNING: If you are a smoker, you might well have the urge to make an attempt to quit now. I'd be the last to prevent you from doing so. However, please be clear that this is not one of the objects of this book, which are threefold:

1 **To establish Easyway as the only sensible way for any smoker to quit.**

2 **To establish that it is the policies of 'the Big 3' that perpetuate smoking and make it difficult, if not impossible, for smokers to break their nicotine addiction.**

3 **To eradicate this scandal as soon as possible. <u>Having achieved objects 1 and 2, to persuade 'the Big 3' to adopt Easyway universally.</u>**

If you are a smoker and your priority is to quit now, I strongly recommend that you attend one of our clinics listed at the back of the book.

In order fully to appreciate the scandal of the current situation, you need to understand how Easyway works.

CHAPTER 9

A BRIEF SYNOPSIS OF EASYWAY

In order to accept that Easyway will be equally effective for any smoker or nicotine addict, you need to know how the method works.

Smokers usually arrive at our clinics in various stages of panic, although they do their best to conceal it. Few are rude enough to say so, but in spite of the fact that the people who recommended the clinic have assured them it is a pleasant experience, their body language tends to give them away. They often sit there with clenched teeth and arms crossed over their chests. The message is unmistakable:

'No way will you be able to help me quit!'

Gradually they begin to relax and unwind and when they leave five hours later they are already happy non-smokers, better equipped to enjoy social occasions, concentrate and handle stress, not having to use willpower, substitutes or other gimmicks, and never having the slightest temptation to smoke again. The method comes with a no-quibble, money-back guarantee and you can even continue to smoke whilst you go through the process of quitting.

DOES THAT SOUND SUCH A BAD DEAL?

Now, allow me to refer back to the tobacco industry, which is under attack from all sides, including 'the Big 3'. Because doctors are the accepted experts on the damage that smoking causes to health, they are also assumed to be the experts on helping smokers to quit.

In fact, their knowledge consists of a mishmash of ignorance, illusion and myth. For years, they have brainwashed smokers to believe it is very difficult to quit and that it takes enormous willpower. Their whole attitude is:

Try this method! If that doesn't work, try another!

This is a perfectly reasonable strategy in the absence of anything better. However, when I discovered a system that would enable any smoker to quit easily, immediately and permanently, they ignored it. When I predicted that the incidence of smoking would be at the same level as snuff-taking is today, I didn't intend that I should cure every smoker personally. I had every reason to believe that my method would be investigated and quickly taken up by 'the Big 3' as official policy. Unbelievably, 23 years later, they are still perpetuating the same ignorance, myths and illusions that keep nicotine addiction flourishing.

It soon became apparent that not only were 'the Big 3' not my allies in the war against addiction but that they were a major obstacle. For every minute of media time I managed to obtain on National No Smoking Days, there were numerous doctors and media articles perpetuating the brainwashing that keeps smokers hooked.

At the beginning of chapter 3, I defined the drug Devastation and asked: '*What does the drug do for you?*' The answer:

ABSOLUTELY NOTHING!

Non-smokers are often at a loss to understand why smokers spend a fortune just for the privilege of breathing cancerous fumes into their lungs, but even they assume that smokers must get some pleasure or advantage from it. It's time we started to explode some of these myths and illusions. Let's start with an extremely important one, the illusion that:

SMOKERS SMOKE BECAUSE THEY CHOOSE TO

CHAPTER 10

ILLUSION – SMOKERS SMOKE BECAUSE THEY CHOOSE TO

One of the problems of curing the world of this disease is that if smokers are indeed in control – as many claim – why would they even want to be cured? I emphasize that I'll put the arguments both for and against, but that you are the final arbiter. I need you to keep an open mind and to use common sense.

Ask someone if they can remember when they actually chose to become a smoker and they will, in all probability, begin to relate the experience of their first experimental cigarettes. Ironically, most smokers remember their first cigarette mainly because it was such an unpleasant experience and they struggled to avoid throwing up or having a coughing fit.

Even more ironic is that this is usually the moment that springs the nicotine trap. We suffer the illusion that smokers smoke because they enjoy smoking. After all, that's what they tell us and why else would they smoke? We are then fooled into believing that whilst we don't enjoy them we won't get hooked, and so we feel secure to continue our experiments.

However, if you point out that you weren't

actually referring to the first experimental cigarettes but to the occasion that the smoker decided to become a permanent smoker – when they would buy their own cigarettes and ensure they always had ample supplies – you will discover that no smoker ever made that decision, although some will deny it!

Perhaps you still need convincing. Smokers will spend hours trying to convince both you and themselves that they are in control, and wax lyrical about the pleasures and advantages they get from being a smoker. Yet ask them if they encourage their children or grandchildren to smoke and you'll get a categorical:

NO WAY!

Doesn't this mean they wish they hadn't fallen into the trap themselves? Still not convinced? Then consider this. Any smoker who has ever made just one, even half-hearted, attempt to quit – and bear in mind that most smokers make several serious attempts – has made a conscious and rational decision that they would rather spend the remainder of their life as a non-smoker. And if they are still smoking, it's not because they choose to, but because they failed to quit.

If you are still not convinced consider this: nobody needs to smoke before trying those first experimental cigarettes. We are perfectly equipped to enjoy meals and other social occasions, to concentrate, answer the phone and handle stress without smoking. Those first cigarettes taste awful and we work hard to learn to inhale without throwing up or having a coughing fit.

The average 20-a-day smoker now spends £100,000 over their lifetime on cigarettes. It wouldn't be so bad if we merely set light to that money. But it's what we actually do with it that's so frightening. We use it to starve every organ of our bodies of oxygen, to poison our lungs and blood vessels with nicotine, carbon monoxide, cancerous fumes and thousands of poisonous compounds. The sheer slavery of being a smoker never seems to dawn on us. We spend half our life moping for a cigarette that society forbids us to smoke and the other half smoking subconsciously, wishing we had no need to. What sort of hobby is it that when you are allowed to do it, you wish you didn't need to, and only when you aren't allowed to smoke does the cigarette seem so precious? It's a lifetime of being despised by other people, but worst of all a lifetime of otherwise intelligent, rational human beings going through life despising themselves!

The biggest idiot on earth wouldn't choose to be a smoker, let alone an intelligent, rational person.

One of the powerful influences that cause ex-smokers to get hooked again is the belief that smokers are in control and smoke because they enjoy it and choose to. Ex-smokers, therefore, envy smokers but fail to realize that all smokers envy them.

I think we have shattered the illusion that smokers smoke because they choose to. It's an exceedingly important one and will enable us to expose another of equal significance:

'THE BIG 3' ATTEMPT TO HELP SMOKERS TO QUIT

CHAPTER 11

ILLUSION – 'THE BIG 3' ATTEMPT TO HELP SMOKERS TO QUIT

For the purpose of quitting, it matters not one iota what type of smoker he or she is, any more than it matters what type of person gets their foot caught in a bear trap. The procedure for releasing them is exactly the same and, providing they follow the instructions, a comparatively painless process. So ladies, please forgive me if, for convenience, I stick to a single male as the example.

Assume that this smoker has been subjected to an average amount of brainwashing, which means he'll believe all or part of a confused concoction of myths about smoking, which may include any of the following:

1 It's an enjoyable habit.

2 It helps you to relax.

3 It relieves stress and boredom.

4 It helps you to concentrate.

5 It gives you confidence.

6 It tastes good.

7 It smells good.

By now, he will have spent several years in the nicotine trap, wishing he'd heeded the warnings of his parents. For some strange reason it won't occur to him that relaxing and stressful situations are complete opposites, as are moments of boredom and concentration. Like the rest of us, he'll just meekly accept that an identical cigarette out of the same packet can give the completely opposite effect to the one smoked an hour earlier. Nor will it occur to him that taste has nothing to do with it. He doesn't eat cigarettes and would be violently sick if he tried to! Smell is simply another red herring. I love the smell of a rose but have never had any desire to set light to the petals and inhale the fumes.

He'll have long lost the illusion that he smokes to feel cool, mature or sophisticated. In all probability, he's already made a couple of half-hearted attempts to quit and, in doing so, has already started off with a feeling of doom and gloom. The moment he extinguishes what he hopes will be his final cigarette, the empty, insecure feeling will kick in. He won't be able to understand it. He'll only know the feeling as: *'I want a cigarette'* and having just primed himself with all the valid reasons why he shouldn't want a cigarette, he won't be able to understand why he still does, will feel stupid and seek help from his doctor.

Imagine a doctor visiting a prison inmate and saying: *'Look old chap, it's damp in here. You run a serious risk of contracting pneumonia and you are clearly under-nourished. Your family is seriously worried about you, so why don't you be sensible and go home!'*

Such a doctor wouldn't only be regarded as stupid but as a patronizing idiot! Are **'the Big 3'** really not aware that smokers have been bombarded by information about the health risks over the past fifty years or so and that if that were going to make them quit, they would already have done so?

Why does it not occur to **'the Big 3'** that smokers do not smoke for the reasons they shouldn't smoke? The real problem is to remove the reasons that they do. Study the seven items listed above. That's some worthwhile package. In fact, they are all illusions, but while smokers continue to believe them, they retain a strong incentive to continue smoking or to start again if they're trying to quit.

The doctor will also have impressed upon the smoker that giving up is not easy and takes willpower. If the man has made previous attempts to give up by using willpower, he will start with a feeling of doom and gloom, try to take his mind off smoking and succeed only in becoming obsessed with it. He'll be constantly reminded of ex-smokers who haven't had a cigarette for ten years but continue to crave them and, even worse, have actually started smoking again after ten years of abstinence. He will also be aware that the doctors' definition of success is to abstain for a whole year. The miracle to me is the number of smokers who actually succeed with a willpower method!

Now let's compare the results achieved by Easyway with those achieved by **'the Big 3'**.

CHAPTER 12

EASYWAY VERSUS 'THE BIG 3'

Since I intend to lay the blame where it belongs – with **'the Big 3'** – I find myself in the unenviable position of still being dependent on **'the Big 3'** to achieve my goal. However, I do have credibility and I fail to see how **'the Big 3'** can accept that I'm the world's leading authority on the subject and yet, at the same time, advocate policies which directly contradict my advice.

Do I resent the attitude of the medical profession? Nothing could be further from the truth. My son is a doctor. I know of no profession more dedicated, hard-working, underpaid, noble or worthy of our respect than our doctors and nurses. I gather that the average GP has something like seven minutes to devote to each patient. Just think of the incredible range of knowledge and skill a doctor has to learn and keep up with. It took me more than thirty years to escape from the nicotine trap and I had the added incentive of my very life depending on it. I've spent the last 23 years doing nothing but honing my one special skill to perfection. I wonder what proportion of a doctor's training time is dedicated to helping smokers quit. Who could possibly blame doctors? It's the system that's wrong. Even if GPs had the time, they wouldn't have the knowledge. This is a very specialized business. It takes a year on average to train a therapist and, in case you think money is our motive, we would be more than happy if the process of education could be speeded up by TV and radio.

Do I blame the politicians? Yes, I do. I estimate that 500,000 smokers have had their lives painfully shortened since Edwina Currie ignored my letter and a like number of youngsters have been lured into the trap. I've no doubt that some were friends or relatives of yours.

Do I blame the media? No way! I've had tremendous support from the media over the years, and I can only offer them my sincere thanks for helping to establish my reputation. In fact, it is with the media that my hopes mainly rest. First, to investigate my method thoroughly, to prove that it's not just the best but the only method for any smoker to adopt; and second, to persuade governments and the medical profession of that fact and spread the good news around the world as quickly as possible.

Perhaps the most frustrating element in my attempt to prove Easyway as the best method is the accusation that I have not subjected the results to so-called clinical trials. Much as I might like to, the thing about clinical trials is that their whole point is to remove what might be called the 'human factor'. Easyway depends on the 'human factor', on people realizing for themselves that they don't need nicotine and, indeed, that they will delight in letting go of their addiction to it.

Medical science, on the other hand, derives its authority by removing anything the patient or doctor might bring to the equation. The idea is to prove what works and what doesn't, regardless of people's culture, their genetic constitution, how they choose to live, how much they want to get better, their trust in their doctor or therapist, or any of a million other human factors.

A clinical trial compares like with like. One arm of the trial consists of people who take a particular drug, and another arm of people who take a placebo, a drug with no active ingredient whatsoever. The critical point is that no one – neither patient nor researcher – knows who is taking what. The idea, as said above, is to remove all possible bias from the process.

You have probably gathered by now that clinical trials can only answer highly specific questions. This gold standard scientific method is all very well and good, and has served medicine well in the past. But it should be pointed out that it only suits drugs. It assumes, and therefore perpetuates the myth, that patients are passive vehicles in which drugs can work their magic. Clinical trials are an entirely inappropriate method of assessing the effectiveness of addiction treatment, not only because the methods used to assess whether the addict has really quit are unreliable but also because they do not allow for any kind of therapy that relies on patients thinking for themselves.

Easyway is not suited to clinical trials because it doesn't work that way. How, for example, could you incorporate a placebo into any such trial? What would that placebo be? In the case of a nicotine patch, for example, the placebo would be a patch without nicotine. But Easyway involves the communication of information to the addict. How would you create a placebo to compare with our clinical sessions? The whole idea is ludicrous.

Having said that, eminent academics are investigating Easyway's remarkable success rate, with all the scientific rigour that can be mustered, in the absence of a placebo. These studies may not be able to compare like with like, but they can, and do, authenticate what we have been saying for years: that Easyway works.

Professor Manfred Neuberger, for example, heads up the Department of Preventive Medicine at the Institute of Environmental Health at Vienna's University of Medicine. The results he has obtained from two studies of Easyway, both in workplace settings, make him a keen advocate of the method.

One study enrolled 515 employees of a steel plant in Austria, who had all taken part in one of my six-hour seminars. After three years, 510 agreed to be interviewed. Of these, 262 (51.4 per cent) were still not smoking. Urine samples were taken to measure their cotinine (a metabolite of nicotine) levels and these suggested the quitters were telling the truth. Professor Neuberger was impressed: *'Every second smoker motivated to participate seems to be able to quit even without medication and to stay abstinent,'* he said in a paper published in the journal, *Addictive Behaviors*, outlining the results.[1]

Another study, again following people who had taken part in a single work-based Easyway seminar, showed a one-year quit rate ranging from 40 per cent (worst-case scenario) to 55 per cent (best-case scenario).[2]

No other method gets even close to this degree of success when subjected to such analysis. Most of the government stop-smoking clinics simply take a smoker's word for it that they have stopped, from questionnaires they send out a few weeks after the course has ended. In the clinics themselves they use a 'smokalizer' to see if someone has smoked. This measures carbon monoxide on the breath, but it only detects if someone has been smoking that day. Testing for cotinine is the most thorough analysis available, because a person would have had to refrain from smoking for three days in order to produce a negative result.

Even with all the limitations of science, Easyway still beats the competition hands down. Why then won't the Government or the medical establishment adopt it?

We have also kept records of the results revealed by the audited accounts of our money-back guarantee. These reveal that year in, year out, our success far exceeds that of any of our rivals. I'm convinced that these are the only reliable results on which comparisons can be based.

Even more frustrating, occasionally it has been falsely claimed in the media that I have started smoking again. While I assure you categorically that this is entirely untrue, I leave you to imagine the effect this has on my mission. Obviously, no one has been able to provide proof. So why is it so frustrating? Because although it is a simple matter to prove that you do smoke, it is impossible to prove that you don't!

I hereby offer a million pounds to anyone who can prove that I smoke and trust that

this action will quash these spiteful rumours.

If even I cannot prove that I don't smoke, how can the results of so-called scientific studies be scientific?

Many doctors encouraged by the pharmaceutical industry, the Government, the medical establishment, the NHS, ASH and QUIT, actually prescribe nicotine in order to help smokers escape from nicotine addiction. They call it:

NICOTINE REPLACEMENT THERAPY (NRT)

I'm referring to products that contain nicotine, such as gum, patches, inhalers and sprays, which claim to help smokers to quit. The expression itself is, of course, a falsehood. The nicotine isn't replaced! On the contrary, it is maintained and there is no therapy.

But the market for nicotine maintenance – now worth more than a billion dollars a year – is so great that people will try anything just to get a slice of it. As if to prove my point, consider this advertisement for a product called Nicogel that I noticed recently. It read:

'Replace your cigarettes today with Nicogel! Nicogel is a revolutionary cigarette replacement. Simply dispense a single press of Nicogel and rub in to the palm of your hands, just as you would hand lotion and in a few minutes you can experience complete cigarette satisfaction that can last for up to four hours.

With increasing numbers of venues now forbidding smoking; the office, your favourite bars and restaurants, the local cinema, trains and even the plane, Nicogel is here to help, designed specifically for you, the smoker, in mind.'

When nicotine gum was followed by nicotine patches, nasal sprays and inhalators, I remember thinking, *'What will the pharmaceutical companies come up with next – a cigarette?'*

I have been saying for some time that the pharmaceutical companies are now in competition with the tobacco companies for the nicotine market. Well, this is the first time I have seen a nicotine product so shamelessly and overtly marketed, not as a means of stopping smoking, but as an alternative to the cigarette. It's even packaged in a small box that looks exactly like a pack of cigarettes. This development further highlights the absurdity of the claims for NRT as an aid to quitting.

Substitution rarely works. Heroin counsellors are finding a similarly limited success rate with the use of alternatives such as methadone. But supposing you discovered that doctors were actually prescribing heroin to cure heroin addiction? Wouldn't you find that absurd? That is exactly what the Government and the NHS, who incidentally agree with me that smoking is nicotine addiction, are doing in relation to nicotine.

THEY ARE ACTUALLY PRESCRIBING NICOTINE TO CURE NICOTINE ADDICTION!

I have gone into great detail to explain why smoking is nothing more nor less than:

ADDICTION TO NICOTINE

To prescribe nicotine in order to cure addiction to nicotine is like saying to a heroin addict: *'Don't smoke heroin, smoking is dangerous, why not just inject it straight into your veins!'*

In fact the whole business of prescribing NRT is a giant confidence trick, motivated by the greed of the pharmaceutical industry and aided and abetted by our Government and the medical establishment. For that reason alone, it ranks with the tobacco industry itself as one of the biggest scandals in history.

I read an interesting article in the *British Medical Journal* recently, by someone not on the payroll of the pharmaceutical industry. It caught my eye because it was entitled 'The NRT cessation charade continues'. The author is an American called John Polito who works as a nicotine cessation educator, which means he is honest about trying to stop the source of the addiction, rather than maintain it. He says, and I quote from that respected journal:

'Imagine a series of studies in which alcoholics being fed alcohol via intravenous bags (which means alcohol is injected directly into the veins) for a period of 3–6 months, were compared with those who had actually quit using all alcohol. Talk about a built-in start! Imagine studies declaring efficacy victory while the bags were still being

used. Imagine billions in profits that could be realized if we could only redefine quitting to mean giving up the bottle or can, while calling intravenous bags of alcohol "medicine" and its use "therapy". And don't forget the advantage we'd realize by the frustrated expectations of those alcoholics who could sense alcohol absence, and the advantage from creating study abstinence definitions that allow a little sip from the bottle now and then. The only thing we'd need to hide would be actual performance.' [3]

The truth is that nicotine maintenance is an extremely profitable business and anything to discredit Easyway by suggesting that I continue to smoke, for example, must add to the demand for NRT products and, therefore, the profits of the companies that make the products. The global NRT market was worth $1.2 billion in 2005. That is $1,200 million or £630 million. And it is growing fast, at around 10 per cent a year. In the UK alone, sales are approaching £100 million a year, more than the total spend in France, Germany, Italy and Spain combined. The main reason for the UK's fascination with NRT products is that the taxpayer, via the NHS, picks up the lion's share of the bill.

One might have thought that if the NHS was spending millions of pounds of taxpayers' money each year by supplying nicotine addicts with nicotine, they would at least have good scientific evidence that NRT works.

WHAT IS THE SCIENTIFIC EVIDENCE?

Clinical trials are only part of the story. Great money and effort may be expended by the pharmaceutical companies setting up the trials but the published results cannot be relied upon. The Healthcare Commission, which is a kind of watchdog of the NHS, assesses the success of the NHS Stop Smoking Clinic by asking people if they are still not smoking four weeks after the date they agreed to stop. They can still be taking nicotine at this point and no one checks they are not smoking.

The Wanless Report of February 2004, commissioned by the Government itself, revealed that a smoker has to quit for only two weeks in the first four to be defined as a success by the NHS Stop Smoking Clinic and concluded that this is an unreliable test of whether a smoker has genuinely stopped. The report says: *'Given the addictive nature of tobacco, only 30 to 40 per cent of smokers truly abstinent at four weeks are likely to be abstinent at one year'.*[4]

As far as medical opinion is concerned, an ex-smoker is generally regarded as a success if he has abstained for at least a whole year. Ignore for now, the fact that the most scientists can do is test for a maximum of three days' abstinence, and that both smokers and ex-smokers, no matter how honest they might be about other aspects of their lives, tend to tell little white lies when discussing their smoking *habits*.

Even if the truth could be proved, why do doctors insist on a year? That sounds rather arbitrary to me. There are numerous cases where the ex-smoker has abstained for a year, thought himself cured and safe, lit up to prove it and got hooked again immediately. In fact, we often have people at our clinics that haven't smoked for several years but seek our help because they fear they'll have to spend the rest of their lives occasionally moping for a cigarette and never knowing whether or not they've really kicked it.

As the effects of NRT are studied in more detail, the nonsense of setting any period of abstinence becomes even more apparent. The vast majority of the clinical studies into the effects of NRT are conducted by doctors who have declared a financial interest in the companies that make NRT products. And the cost of the studies, which often runs into millions of pounds, is picked up by the pharmaceutical companies themselves because public health budgets don't have that kind of money.

One study, published in the journal, *Tobacco Control*, which is part of the BMJ Publishing Group, tried to establish how effective NRT is over the long haul.[5] It was a meta-analysis, which looks at work that has already been done in this area. These researchers focused on 12 trials that had announced results after one year and then were followed up after a further two to eight years. The results are interesting.

As we know, a clinical trial must compare the drug in question, in this case nicotine, with a placebo, which has no active ingredient whatsoever. If a trial was to assess nicotine patches, for example, the placebo would be a plaster that looked like a nicotine patch. No one, neither researcher nor smoker, knows who is on NRT or placebo.

In these 12 trials, a total of 2,408 people were on

NRT products and 2,384 on a placebo. The results showed that three in every ten people who claimed to have stopped at 12 months, admitted to starting again. What the authors of the study concluded from this was: *'Because the long-term benefit of NRT is modest, tobacco dependence treatment might be better viewed as a chronic disorder, requiring repeated episodes of treatment.'*

Rather than look at other methods, such as Easyway, or question the farce of feeding nicotine addiction with nicotine, the authors seem to be suggesting that more money should be spent on nicotine products. Even more scandalous, what this study also shows and wasn't flagged up by the authors (who admit to having taken money from the drugs companies), is that NRT becomes even **less** effective over time.

On average, the analysis shows that after a year 18 per cent of people said they were still not smoking using NRT; a figure that had whittled down to 12 per cent over eight years. For those on placebo, 10 per cent had quit cigarettes after a year; going down to 8 per cent over the longer term. This translates to a 'success' for NRT over placebo of 8 per cent at 12 months and 4 per cent over the long haul.

However, the largest and most recent study that the authors looked at (completed in 2003 and involving 815 smokers), more than halves this so-called success rate and suggests that people get used to NRT. Once the novelty has worn off, in other words, it is used as simply another source of nicotine, a convenient aid for those occasions where it is antisocial to smoke, or as a free alternative to cigarettes – courtesy of the NHS!

This study found that after a year 11 per cent were not smoking having used NRT. After eight years, that had reduced to 6 per cent. In the placebo group, 8 per cent had quit after a year and 4 per cent over the long term. The net gain from using NRT was, therefore, just 3 per cent at 12 months and just 2 per cent over the full term.

But the main thing that such studies demonstrate is one of the major problems of any willpower system. When you're trying to *give up*, how do you know when you've succeeded? It's obvious that the clients attending our clinics haven't even pondered the question, and when prompted to do so come up with a variety of answers:

1 **'I know if I could just manage a whole day without one, I'd never smoke again!'**

'Problem solved! I'll lock you up for 24 hours with food, drink but no cigarettes.'

'I don't think that will work.'

'I'm sure it wouldn't.'

2 **'When I stop thinking about smoking.'**

'How can you ever stop thinking about smoking? It's like a restless night – the more you try to sleep, the worse it gets.

'If you try *not* to think about smoking you will

guarantee that your mind will become obsessed with nothing else.'

3 **'When I can enjoy a meal, a drink, socializing or answer the phone, cope with a trauma (the list is endless), without a cigarette.'**

'And how long will that be?'

'I don't know! But I've managed to hold out for six weeks and I intend to stick in there.'

Do you begin to see the problem? Suppose someone does manage to answer the phone without even thinking of having a cigarette, or achieves one of those other goals, he'll obviously be delighted, but that doesn't guarantee he won't be tempted the next time. In any event, terms like 'holding out' and 'sticking in there', though a great tribute to his determination, do not indicate a particularly pleasant experience.

They do go some way, however, to explaining why people who have quit with Easyway have such a different attitude from those who have stopped by using other methods. Because Easyway removes the feeling of deprivation, Easyway stoppers are happy stoppers.

Happy stoppers are also less likely to start again than those using sheer willpower. So what exactly are all those miserable stoics actually trying to achieve? Perhaps you think the answer is obvious:

NEVER TO SMOKE AGAIN

So we build up our reserves, pick the day and make a solemn vow never to smoke again and extinguish what we hope will be our last cigarette. No sooner have we done so than the withdrawal pangs kick in. To our brains this means:

'I NEED OR WANT A CIGARETTE!'

So we start to crave a cigarette and know that a cigarette will end the craving. But we've vowed to *give up* and won't allow ourselves to have one. This makes us feel deprived and miserable. And what do smokers do when they feel depressed? That's right – they have a cigarette. Now their need is greater, but they still can't have one.

I've said the withdrawal pangs from nicotine are almost imperceptible and indistinguishable from hunger and normal stress. There is no physical pain but the cause is physical.

DON'T UNDERESTIMATE THE EFFECT IT CAN HAVE!

Remember times when you were very hungry and were kept waiting another two hours for your meal? Remember how angry and irritable it made you feel? Accept that prolonged hunger will force people to eat worms, bugs and rats, and that otherwise normal and decent people have even turned to cannibalism.

This will perhaps help non-smokers understand the true agony that many smokers suffer when trying to *give up* with the help of willpower methods. However, it occurs to me that I'm probably convincing you that it's difficult to quit. I will explain:

HOW EASYWAY REVERSES THE DIFFICULTIES OF QUITTING

Before doing so, we need to pass on to Part 3 – Frustration. I emphasize that as far as my own smoking is concerned, that moment of exaltation on 15 July 1983 has never dimmed and never will. The frustration was in my attempts to gain credibility. Oh, the network of clinics was expanding at an incredible rate and so were book sales, but frustrations had started to creep in. Some clients who had successfully quit for several months, or even years, were getting hooked again and returning to the clinic. Then a completely unfounded rumour went around that I was smoking again. This was a real body blow.

However, the real cruncher came from the event that I fully expected would establish Easyway worldwide as the only method to quit. I had been invited by Professor Judith Mackay to give a lecture at the Tenth World Conference on Tobacco or Health, held in 1997 in Beijing. At that time, Judith had already been identified by the tobacco companies as the second most dangerous person in the world. She went on to become Senior Policy Advisor on tobacco control to the World Health Organization (WHO).

It seemed a heaven-sent opportunity. I was even lucky enough to be the last to lecture. All week I sat through stories of woe, practically every one of which ended with the words:

WE NEED MORE RESEARCH!

I couldn't wait to explain to all these dedicated men and women that they didn't need more research and that I had already discovered what they were all searching for. Not one even bothered to attend my lecture. It hadn't occurred to me that the conference had been sponsored by the companies that sell nicotine patches and gum. I hadn't realized then just how extraordinarily wealthy these companies are and how they are able to dominate the entire scientific establishment.

At the time of writing, Nicorette gum, for example, was produced by Pharmacia, which is owned by Pfizer, the world's number one drugs company. This single company, according to Jacky Law's excellent book *Big Pharma*, was worth $238.8 billion in April 2004. In 2003, it had sales of $40 billion and more than a billion prescriptions were written for its products.

In fact, just ten pharmaceutical companies earned no less than $205 billion (£107 billion) in 2004.[6] That is just $10 billion less than the entire gross domestic product of Denmark in that same year. Denmark is not an underdeveloped country; it is an affluent democratic nation with 5.4 million people. Pharmaceutical companies, on the other hand, are run by a number you could probably count on a couple of hands. Moreover, these powerful people are legally obliged to act in the best interests of their shareholders. **THEY DO**

WHATEVER THEY CAN GET AWAY WITH!

You might think there would be rules to stop these massive 'druggernauts' acting in their own best interests when millions of lives are at stake. Of course there are. But these rules, and the people who interpret them on our behalf, have come in for a lot of high-level criticism lately. The report of the UK's 2004 parliamentary inquiry into the influence of the pharmaceutical industry said:

'The Department of Health has, for too long, optimistic-ally assumed that the interests of health and of industry are one... This may reflect the fact that the Department sponsors the industry as well as looking after health. The result is that the industry has been left to its own devices for too long.' [7]

It went on to describe the grip 'Big Pharma' has on our healthcare services:

'The industry affects every level of healthcare provision, from the drugs that are initially discovered and developed through clinical trials, to the promotion of drugs to the prescriber and the patient groups, to the prescription of medicines and the compilation of clinical guidelines.' [8]

Commercial enterprise is no bad thing, of course. But every country in the world recognizes that the private interests in the medicines business must be curtailed to protect the natural vulnerability of the public, especially in markets where single drugs can earn more than $10 billion a year. That is why it was disturbing to hear evidence that private interests now dictate how the NHS is run.

The editor of the UK medical journal, the *Lancet*, Dr Richard Horton, told the inquiry:

'The pharmaceutical industry has been enormously successful at inter-digitalizing itself in the usual process of healthcare in the UK. It provides equipment, services, buildings, facilities and, of course, hospitality. At almost every level of NHS care provision, the pharmaceutical industry shapes the agenda and the practice of medicine.' [9]

Becoming more aware about the colossal wealth of the global pharmaceutical companies puts everything in a different light – particularly if it is to do with persuading people to take more medicines. The Medicines Partnership is a good example of this. It is an initiative set up by the Department of Health to address the fact that up to 80 per cent of patients don't take their medicines properly. [10]

Pharmaceutical companies, as it happens, are also keen that patients should take more medicines, because that means more sales. London GP Dr Iona Heath shares my fears that we are becoming so over-medicalized that we hardly recognize it any more. She acknowledges the good intentions behind the Medicines Partnership but points out that its website states that, at any one time, seven in ten of the UK population are taking medicine to treat or prevent ill health: *'This statement is made with no further comment,'* she says, *'but how can this level of drug taking be appropriate in a population that, by all objective measures, is healthier than ever before in history?'* [11]

It is rare to find someone who talks sense in the medicines business. Everyone else seems to want as many people as possible on as many drugs as possible. As far as nicotine is concerned, that means getting it into the body via nicotine products, so that nicotine addicts can still get their fix even when they are not able to smoke. In this way they are helped to perpetuate their addiction.

If it sounds like a scandal, that is because it is a scandal. The MPs, in their inquiry into the workings of the industry, also went to great lengths to highlight the excellent medical research that companies do; and their contribution to the national economy in terms of well paid jobs and export earnings. Their concerns were all to do with the **extent** of their influence:

'In some circumstances, one particular item of influence may be of relatively little importance,' they said in their report. *'Only when it is viewed as part of a larger package of influences is the true effect of the companies' activity recognized and the potential for distortion seen.'* [12]

This insight into the workings of this important industry was illuminating as far as understanding why Easyway wasn't being celebrated around the world. Pharmaceutical companies use their vast wealth to fund conferences into tobacco and nicotine. They pay doctors to do the clinical studies and they even define what success means in those studies. They aren't interested in getting people off nicotine. How can they be, if their first obligation is to their shareholders and they are making a fortune by selling nicotine? As with all companies, that means expanding markets.

In fact, as noted earlier, the makers of so-called Nicotine Replacement Therapy (NRT) are in competition with the tobacco companies for the nicotine-addicted market.

I was recently in a restaurant and noticed the lady at the next table was chewing on nicotine gum. I asked her whether she was trying to stop smoking. She said, *'No. I just use this to tide me over until I can have another cigarette.'*

Indeed this is one way NRT is being marketed nowadays. The No Smoking signs on the London Underground have an advertisement under them, which reads:

'At times like this, it needn't be hell with Nicotinelle.'

Note: *'At times like this'* – NRT is now being increasingly marketed, and increasingly used, not as a way of stopping but as a way of getting through the periods when one cannot smoke: for example, in restaurants, on planes, and so on.

Indeed, nicotine gum was originally invented by the Swedish to help smoking submariners get through the periods when they could not smoke in the submarines, not as a means of stopping.

The very term Nicotine Replacement Therapy is a misnomer. Nicotine is not being replaced and there is nothing therapeutic about it. It should be called Nicotine Continuation Treatment. It is not in the interests of the pharmaceutical companies to cure nicotine addiction – they are selling nicotine!

The term Nicotine Replacement Therapy is not only a falsehood, but the whole theory on which it is sold to the public is based on two incorrect facts. The supposition is that when you try to *give up* smoking you have two powerful enemies to defeat:

1　To break the habit.

2　To withstand the terrible physical withdrawal pangs from nicotine.

It sounds logical. If you have two powerful enemies to defeat, better to tackle them one at a time. The idea is that you first *give up* smoking and whilst you are breaking the habit, keep your brain and body addicted to nicotine by using the nicotine product. Then the theory is that once you've broken the habit you gradually wean yourself off the nicotine.

Let's suppose for a moment that the two assumptions on which the strategy is based are correct. The same effect could be achieved by weaning yourself off both the habit and the terrible physical withdrawal pangs in the first place by gradually cutting down, which would cost the ex-smoker nothing. However, as most smokers have already found, in the same way that a so-called alcoholic can't just cut down their intake of alcohol, cutting down doesn't work.

In fact both the 'habit' and 'nicotine withdrawal' assumptions are false. I've also explained that the actual withdrawal pangs from nicotine are so mild that smokers only know them as:

'I WANT OR NEED A CIGARETTE!'

It is true that smokers attempting to *give up* when using the methods that **'the Big 3'** advocate often suffer considerable misery and depression. But this is purely mental, the sort of panic a smoker suffers when he's running low on cigarettes and will venture out late at night in search of an all-night garage. With physical pain, you have to ask yourself:

'WHERE DOES IT ACTUALLY HURT?'

The second fallacy is that the so-called *habit* is hard to break. The fact is that smoking is not a *habit*, it's an addiction and that provided you have removed the illusions which make part of your brain wish to continue to smoke, the so-called *habit* is easy to break. Your frame of mind becomes not so much:

'I MUSN'T SMOKE EVER AGAIN!'

as:

'ISN'T IT GREAT! I DON'T EVER NEED

OR WANT TO SMOKE AGAIN!'

In fact, all substitutes make it harder to quit. If you even search for a substitute, what you will actually be saying to yourself is:

*'I'M MAKING A GENUINE SACRIFICE,
I NEED SOMETHING TO TAKE ITS PLACE'*

That will establish in your mind the idea that you have made a genuine sacrifice. With Easyway you see the situation as it really is, you've given up:

ABSOLUTELY NOTHING!

When you get over a bout of flu, do you search for another disease to take its place?

In fact, there are two genuine adversaries to defeat when you quit smoking. The one that causes the misery and makes it difficult is the 'big monster'. Fortunately, Easyway removes the craving even before extinguishing the final cigarette. How do we defeat the 'little monster'? Once you cut off the supply of nicotine, he'll die of starvation in just a few days. Remember the feeling is almost imperceptible and we only know it as:

'I NEED OR WANT A CIGARETTE!'

See it instead as it really is – the death throes of the 'little monster' – and you can rejoice that you will soon be free of it and never have to suffer it again.

Any substitute containing nicotine is doubly bad because it prolongs the life of both monsters. Thousands of ex-smokers are addicted to NRT products and we often have clients attend our clinics to be cured of that addiction.

I can remember when doing National Service in the Royal Air Force, having frequent breaks 'for a smoke'. Smoking housewives will punctuate their day with regular breaks for a 'ciggy'. This can create the feeling of a void when they try to quit. It is important to be aware that smoking never, ever fills a void; on the contrary, it creates one. Even so, after she has quit smoking at those regular times when she had the break for a cigarette, she can get the feeling that she's being deprived of her little reward. I suggest two ways to avoid this problem.

Usually the break was taken because she needed a cigarette not because she needed a break, so the answer is to cut out the break and enjoy a more productive day. However, if you want to maintain the ritual, wear a pair of shoes one size too small whilst you are working and remove them during your coffee break. Either way, you'll find the problem will soon resolve itself. The best way to get such breaks in perspective is to observe smokers standing in the cold outside non-smoking offices in a vain attempt to satisfy the insatiable 'little monster'.

Seriously though, the only benefit any smoker ever gets from a cigarette break is from the break itself, not from the cigarette. As a non-smoker it's wonderful to choose when to have a break rather than, in the past as a smoker, TO HAVE to take one because you're desperate for a cigarette.

The frustration I mentioned earlier had crept up on me, rather as Devastation had, but just as Easyway removed my devastation overnight, I have every belief that this book will remove:

FRUSTRATION

PART 3

FRUSTRATION

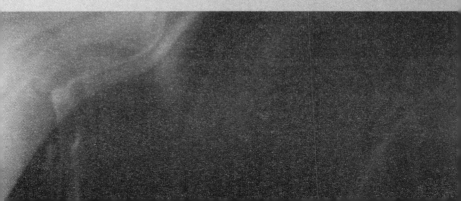

CHAPTER 13

HOW EASYWAY REVERSES THE DIFFICULTIES OF QUITTING

I have explained that the doctors' method consists of telling smokers what they already know:

1 You are poisoning your body and risking truly horrific diseases.

2 You are spending a small fortune for the privilege of doing so.

3 It's a filthy disgusting *habit!*

In spite of all the evidence that we've been inundated with over the past fifty years, it seems certain smokers refuse to accept that smoking damages their health. You've probably noticed that it's usually the younger ones. Ironically, far too many heavy, long-term smokers with obvious and permanent smoker's coughs make the same claim, but I suspect their reasons are the same as mine: the belief that they could never become a happy non-smoker.

I think it is generally agreed that the doctors'

points are valid. However, as I've already pointed out, we do not smoke for the reasons we shouldn't smoke.

In chapter 11, I referred to the real problem, the reasons that cause youngsters to fall into the trap and prevent them from escaping. For convenience, I will repeat them:

1 It's enjoyable and sociable in some crowds.

2 It helps you to relax.

3 It relieves stress and boredom.

4 It helps you to concentrate.

5 It gives you confidence.

6 It tastes good.

7 It smells good.

The list is far from exhaustive. For example, many smokers will give other reasons, such as: *'It's just habit'*, or *'I've got an addictive personality'*. However, these strike me as not so much reasons for smoking but excuses for having failed to *give up*.

So imagine this permanent tug-of-war that goes on in every smoker's mind. On one side, the baddies: the health risks, the money, the slavery and so on. On the other side, the pleasure: the crutch and the rest. If any smoker were to sit down and allocate points to each item and then tot up the totals on each side of the argument, his rational answer would be to quit.

Why? Because every smoker knows they never intended to become a regular smoker and that they neither needed nor wanted cigarettes before they started experimenting. In truth, it is not a tug-of-war between the advantages and disadvantages of being a smoker, but a tug-of-war of fear. On one side, fear of the consequences of continuing to smoke, such as the health scares, the wasted money and so on. On the other side, fear of life without our little crutch or pleasure. Smokers accept that they begin to feel insecure without cigarettes. They also feel they can no longer enjoy social occasions or handle stress without a cigarette and believe this is because they get some genuine pleasure or support from smoking.

In fact, nobody ever gets any genuine pleasure or support from smoking. If you are a smoker, light one up now, take six deep consecutive puffs and ask yourself whether you are really enjoying breathing those filthy cancerous fumes into your lungs. All the smoker ever enjoys is trying to satisfy the craving. What it amounts to is not that the smoker enjoys smoking the cigarettes, but that he can't enjoy life without them.

This is why so much of our smoking is done subconsciously. Even the lighting up becomes automatic and most smokers will admit that they only enjoy about two of the twenty or so they average each day. Unless, of course, they are trying to cut down, when their whole lives become dominated by the next cigarette.

If, every time you smoked a cigarette, you were

consciously aware of inhaling filthy, cancerous fumes into your lungs; of a time-bomb ticking away that this particular cigarette might trigger off; and of fact that you were paying a small fortune for the privilege; then even the illusion of pleasure would disappear. This is why smokers block their minds to the reality, hoping that one day – by some miracle – they will quit. Unfortunately, drug addiction doesn't work that way: the more the drug drags you down, the more dependent you feel on it.

Why do smokers continue to smoke when their rational brains tell them to *give up*? Because these are the fears of the future. Youngsters know they won't get lung cancer today. When father, who is puffing away himself, pleads with his children:

'Why don't you quit before you get hooked?'

He's likely to get the response:

'You're the one who needs to quit! Have you listened to your chest lately?'

The fear of life without cigarettes begins the moment you decide to make an attempt to stop. Do I have the willpower? Will I enjoy social occasions? Will I be able to concentrate? Will I be one of those whinging ex-smokers and have to spend the rest of my life resisting temptation? Is it the right time? I'm under too much pressure at the moment. My holiday's coming up; I don't think I could enjoy it without smoking and so on and so on.

If we smoke to relax and concentrate and to relieve boredom and stress, what other times are left? This is all part of the ingenuity of the confidence trick. It's designed to trap us with just one cigarette and keep us trapped until it kills us.

Incidentally, it might not have occurred to you that both sides of the tug-of-war of fear are caused by smoking. Non-smokers don't suffer from either. Smokers suffer from both sides throughout their smoking lives.

Easyway will prove all the so-called goodies are illusions. Not only does smoking not relax you or help you concentrate, or relieve stress or boredom, but it does the complete opposite. And I must emphasize that the main stresses it causes are in addition to the items included on the doctors' baddie list.

We've already dispelled some of these illusions. Let's get on with shattering some more. Let's start with the correct answer to the question:

WHAT ARE WE TRYING TO ACHIEVE?

CHAPTER 14

WHAT ARE WE TRYING TO ACHIEVE?

The answer may seem obvious:

NEVER TO SMOKE AGAIN

Like most facts about the nicotine trap, that answer might seem obvious, but it is wrong. With the willpower method, we force ourselves into a self-imposed tantrum, like a child deprived of its sweets. We spend the next few weeks, months or years craving a cigarette but not allowing ourselves to have one, desperately hoping that if we can stick it out long enough, eventually we'll wake up with a feeling of:

FANTASTIC! I'VE KICKED IT! I'M FREE!

THAT FEELING IS WHAT WE ARE TRYING TO ACHIEVE

Another myth is that the ex-smoker has no choice but to continue to crave cigarettes, particularly in the first few days when he's trying to break the *habit*.

In chapter 6, I said it is strictly incorrect to describe the withdrawal pangs of nicotine as 'craving a cigarette'. Allow me to explain why. That empty, insecure feeling which triggers the thought:

'I NEED OR WANT A CIGARETTE!'

is purely physical. It is also almost imperceptible and occurs when the nicotine level in the bloodstream falls below a certain level. I call that the 'little monster'. It is like a tapeworm in your stomach that feeds on nicotine. Why 'little'? Because it's so imperceptible that smokers don't even realize it's the only true reason they light their next cigarette and it gets no worse when smokers extinguish their final cigarette.

Incidentally, have you ever noticed the careful distinction a smoker will place between the words 'need' and 'want'? Observe a lone smoker at a dinner party, fiddling with his cigarette packet and lighter, whilst he politely waits for the remaining guests to finish their meal. Ask him if he *needs* a cigarette. The reply will usually be something like: *'I don't need one, but I would enjoy one.'* 'Enjoy' means he's in control. 'Need' means he's an addict.

When the 'little monster' sends its signal to the brain, the smoker instinctively knows a cigarette will immediately relieve the feeling and so starts to crave one. Now, you must admit it is somewhat stupid to make a vow one day that you never want to smoke another cigarette, only to then spend the next few days actually craving one. I refer to the craving as the 'big monster' because this is the great trauma smokers go through when trying to *give up* using willpower methods.

If your object is to quit for a year and you manage to do so, at least you know you've achieved it – although that's no guarantee you'll remain a non-smoker for life. But if your objective is never to smoke again, you'll have to spend the rest of your life waiting to find out if you succeed. You'll be waiting not to smoke again which means you're actually waiting and hoping for:

NOTHING TO HAPPEN!

This is what many ex-smokers actually do. And remember, they are the lucky ones. Why not use Easyway and get free immediately?

The true difference between a smoker and a non-smoker is not that one smokes and the other doesn't; it's that a non-smoker has neither any need nor any desire to smoke and looks upon smokers with genuine pity rather than envy.

The beautiful truth is that once smokers understand the nicotine trap, they are in control of the craving and need never crave another cigarette after extinguishing what they know will be their final cigarette. By removing all the illusions beforehand, Easyway enables the smoker to have that immediate feeling of:

FANTASTIC! I'M FREE!

There is no feeling of doom or gloom, but rather a

feeling of exaltation at having been released from that addiction to Devastation.

Now let's remove some more illusions. Imagine that list of illusions as the official guide to escaping from the smoking maze. Little wonder that smokers who don't understand the nature of the illusion find it difficult to escape and millions of other people continue to fall into the trap! Let's now shatter the illusion that:

JUST ONE CIGARETTE WON'T HOOK YOU

CHAPTER 15

ILLUSION – JUST ONE CIGARETTE WON'T HOOK YOU

We'll see. One thing's already for sure:

IF YOU DON'T HAVE AN EXPERIMENTAL CIGARETTE

YOU CAN'T GET HOOKED!

It is usually insects that eat plants. But there are some plants which supplement their diets by devouring insects. A particularly fascinating variety is the pitcher plant. As its name suggests it is shaped like a pitcher.

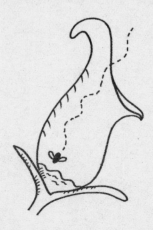

The plant sends out an aroma that flying insects find irresistible. The upper inside leaves of the plant contain hairs, which are covered with delicious nectar. The insect alights and starts feasting on the nectar.

At the bottom of the plant is a pool of digestive juices, in which other insects are floating in various stages of being digested. This should send out warning signals to the insect feasting above. But being so absorbed in his banquet he shows no concern. And why should he? After all, he has wings and can fly off whenever he chooses to.

He is gradually moving in one direction only: downwards. When he has completed gorging himself, he tries to fly away. But the nectar is very sticky and, just as it's impossible to eat jam on toast without coating your fingers with sticky stuff, so the insect's wings and legs get stuck. The more it struggles, the worse the situation becomes. The walls of the plant have imperceptibly steepened and the restraining hairs are rapidly disappearing. The inevitable result:

One more for the pot!

At what stage was the insect trapped? When it found it couldn't fly away? No, that was the stage it realized it was trapped. The insect was trapped the moment it responded to its natural instincts. The plant fooled it into believing it was in control. The truth is that the plant was controlling it from the moment it got a whiff of the nectar. And the plant never even lost a drop of its precious bait. In the same way, the youngster falls into the nicotine trap the moment he decides to try that first experimental cigarette.

Why doesn't every youngster get hooked? There are many reasons. Some are sensible enough not to experiment. Others can't afford to. The most important influence is not your parents but the crowd you mix or work with. Many find their lungs can't cope with the learning process. But let's not waste time worrying about the ones who escape the trap. We should shatter the illusion that has, undoubtedly, the most powerful effect on helping nicotine addiction to survive:

SMOKING IS A HABIT

CHAPTER 16

ILLUSION – SMOKING IS A HABIT

First, let's explode a closely associated illusion that tends to confuse the situation:

HABITS ARE DIFFICULT TO BREAK

Are habits difficult to break? All my life I've been in the habit of driving on the left. When I drive on the continent or in the USA, I have no difficulty whatsoever in driving on the right. The main reason we believe habits are difficult to break is because we've been brainwashed to believe smoking is a habit. It is a fact that smokers generally find it difficult to *give up* but this isn't because smoking is a habit.

Even if it were, if you decide that you never want to smoke again, why should it be difficult? After all no one can force you to smoke. You don't even have to take any positive action; you simply don't light another cigarette. What could be easier? The answer the so-called experts give is the terrible withdrawal pangs from nicotine. Forget for the moment that their argument supports mine, that is, smoking is addiction to nicotine and not habit. Let's remove another common illusion:

SMOKERS SUFFER AWFUL WITHDRAWAL PANGS WHEN THEY QUIT!

I confess this was a great mystery to me when I extinguished my final cigarette on 15 July 1983. I knew I would never smoke again but how could I go 'cold turkey' straight from chain smoking, without suffering the misery I'd experienced on my previous attempts? It wasn't until I re-examined those attempts and asked myself where the actual pain was, that I realized there wasn't any.

If you hit your thumb hard with a hammer, you might eventually forget whether it was your right or left thumb, but you'll never forget it was your thumb. What I could remember was banging my head against the wall, hoping my wife would say:

'Look, if it's that bad, for goodness sake have a cigarette!'

I'd been acting like a child having a tantrum. I was in no physical pain, I just wanted a cigarette. I was really just trying to save face. I hadn't aborted the attempt. I could now blame my wife. What pathetic creatures that little cigarette can reduce us to!

Smokers who can't last an hour during the day without a cigarette can sleep eight hours without withdrawal and they don't wake up in any pain. In fact, since smoking became antisocial, many smokers leave the bedroom before they light up. Others will eat breakfast first. They aren't suffering terrible withdrawal pangs, they aren't even in a panic, but they are looking forward to the first cigarette of the day. However, if when they tried to light it you were to snatch it away, then you'd see panic and be lucky to get away without a broken arm.

If there are severe withdrawal pangs, how come the vast majority of our clients report that they don't suffer them? Does that mean some of them do? Bear in mind that in just five hours we are attempting to reverse a lifetime of brainwashing. Some people aren't capable of making the transition in just one session. Usually, the conversation goes something like this:

Client: *You told me there would be no bad withdrawal pangs but I'm in agony.*

Therapist: Where does it hurt?

Client: *Nowhere in particular but I'm climbing the wall!*

Therapist: Can you describe the symptoms?

Client: *I just want a cigarette.*

In such cases, a second session usually solves the problem. Can you see the extent of the brainwashing?

At other times the conversation goes like this:

Client: *You told me there would be no bad withdrawal pangs but I'm climbing the wall.*

Therapist: Can you describe the symptoms?

Client: *I'm in a cold sweat. It's like having flu.*

Therapist: Has your doctor diagnosed this as nicotine withdrawal?

Client: *I haven't consulted him.*

Flu is a very unpleasant thing to have, but we are perfectly able to handle it. In fact, if somebody had said to me: *'I'll release you from the nicotine prison provided you suffer flu for a month'*, I'd have leapt at the opportunity.

Does this mean the withdrawal pangs can be like flu? Only if you haven't followed the instructions.

Now that we've dealt with the illusion of the terrible withdrawal pangs, we can concentrate on shattering the illusion:

SMOKING IS A HABIT

We have a chicken-and-egg situation here, except that, with the use of a little common sense, we can solve it. In order to become a habit, a certain type of behaviour must be repeated. How often would you say one needed to repeat behaviour before it becomes a habit? Let's not be finicky and, for the sake of argument, say that if you repeat a certain form of behaviour five or more times, it becomes a *habit*.

A smoker certainly doesn't smoke his first cigarette out of habit, or the second, or the third. So no one starts smoking out of habit. It works the other way around. It only seems to become a habit because the smoker starts smoking regularly. You might be asking yourself what difference it makes. Please bear with me. We are near the crux of the matter and it is vital that you know whether people smoke out of habit or because they are addicted to nicotine, as I have suggested.

In fact, we are never controlled by habits. Certain behaviour can become habitual but we are normally in control, as in the example of which side of the road we choose to drive. Some repeated behaviour, such as nail-biting, we might wish we didn't do. However, there is always a reason for repeated behaviour and that reason is not because it's a habit. The fact that we don't understand the reason doesn't alter the fact.

Conclusion:

WE DON'T SMOKE OUT OF HABIT

If we did, it would be just as easy to break the habit as to start it.

We have reached a crucial stage in understanding exactly why the tactics of the 'Big 3' tend to keep smokers hooked and, even when they do manage to escape, get them hooked again.

I have described that stage during an attempt to *give up* on a willpower method, when, after the final cigarette has been extinguished, the 'little monster' gets hungry and the 'big monster' starts to crave a cigarette. The ex-smoker has been brainwashed from birth to believe smoking is a habit and the pattern of his own addiction has reinforced that brainwashing. Now he's desperately using willpower in an attempt to break the *habit*. However, there are several factors working against him.

I've already mentioned that the withdrawal pangs from nicotine are indistinguishable from normal stress. The ex-smoker not only has the 'little monster' to contend with, but the willpower method itself causes stress and tension. If the ex-smoker also happens to be hungry, all three factors will be blamed on the fact he's not allowed to smoke.

What would you say were the favourite cigarettes for most smokers? The one after a meal is usually high on the list. Some smokers actually claim that the cigarette after a meal tastes better than others. Ignore for a moment the fact that we don't eat cigarettes – if we did we'd be violently sick – how can an otherwise intelligent person come to the conclusion that an identical cigarette out of the same packet actually tastes different from another? I think we have disposed of that particular illusion.

Another favourite for many smokers is that first cigarette of the day, even though it seems to taste worse than the others. Others include: the first one after leaving work, after sex, after exercise, after a journey on public transport, after a flight and after the cinema. In fact, all 'favourite' cigarettes follow a period of abstinence.

This isn't just coincidence. All any smoker ever enjoys when lighting up is not the cigarette itself but satisfying the 'little monster'. Just like a hunger for food, the longer you suffer it, the greater the illusion of pleasure once you are allowed to satisfy the empty, insecure feeling.

The natural tendency is to build a resistance to all poisons. Imagine you'd created an incredible variety of species. How would you protect them from poisoning themselves? One way would be to do what Mother Nature did, invent an ingenious device called 'smell'. Probably the most nutritious food for human consumption is fresh fruit. It looks good, feels good, smells good and tastes good. So sophisticated is the system that, if fruit putrefies, it now looks rotten, smells rotten, feels rotten and tastes rotten.

When we experiment with the first cigarettes, the coughing and nausea is our body's way of warning us:

YOU ARE FEEDING ME POISON! PLEASE STOP DOING IT!

If we fail to heed the warning, our bodies assume we have no choice but to continue to ingest it and we build a tolerance to the foul taste and smell. We refer to such tastes as 'acquired' tastes. It's not so much that we've acquired the taste, as built a resistance to it. It's a bit like working on a pig farm. You get used to the smell of the pigs and they get used to your smell. But don't be surprised if your friends are less tolerant.

However, acquired taste is a double-edged sword. While it means you can tolerate the poisoning better, it also means you only partially relieve the withdrawal pangs. So the natural tendency of all drug addiction is to increase the dose. Eventually, the smoker will reach what I refer to as the 'critical point'. This is the stage when you feel that your intake is beginning to affect your health. And this is often the time when we make a serious effort to quit, usually beginning with an attempt to cut down.

Why do I call it the 'critical point'? Because the smoker has reached an unenviable position: the point whereby at one and the same time part of his brain wishes he could smoke less and another wants to smoke more.

We know that when we first started smoking it was at nothing like our present level. Because we have been brainwashed to believe smoking is a *habit*, we assume that we have merely got into the habit of smoking too much. We think: *'If I can cut down to five a day for the next ten days, I'll soon get back into the habit of only wanting five a day.'*

Unfortunately, it's not *habit* but drug *addiction* and the tendency with drugs is to want more and more, not less and less. The moment you try to cut down or restrict your intake for any reason, terrible things happen. Prior to cutting down, whenever the 'little monster' cries out for satisfaction you can light up immediately. However, if you're cutting down you now have to wait until your next cigarette is due.

I lost count of the number of times I tried to cut down. None of my attempts worked, although at the time the logic seemed sound. I think the best example of the futility of cutting down was provided by one of my early clients.

This young housewife was on 40 a day and decided it would be no great sacrifice just to cut out one ciga-rette each day and, provided she did that, she would end up a non-smoker.

She eventually got down to one a day but couldn't get rid of the last one. This is how she described her life:

'I'd get my husband off to work and the children off to school and then sit down to enjoy my cigarette. Then I'd think: "No! I'll do the washing up first." Then I'd think: "I'll do the ironing first." All day I'd be dangling this carrot in front of my nose and I would eventually smoke it before I collected the children from school.'

This poor lady was trying to *give up* smoking but all she succeeded in doing was convincing herself that the most precious thing on earth was a cigarette. Now her entire life was being dominated by the next cigarette.

Smoking is drug addiction, not habit. In order to cut down, you'd need to apply willpower and discipline for the rest of your life. With Easyway, quitting is easy and needs no willpower. If you haven't got the willpower to quit, no way could you cut down for the rest of your life.

Heavy smokers tend to envy casual smokers and smokers who are cutting down. Why? Why do smokers always boast about how little they smoke? Why do they make statements like: *'Do you know I can go a whole week without a cigarette and it doesn't bother me!'* I can do the same with carrots but find no need to boast about it. But if it truly doesn't bother them not to smoke, then:

WHY BOTHER SMOKING AT ALL?

Believe me, there is no such thing as a happy smoker. Because these smokers tell us they are happy and in control, we believe them. So how do they manage to limit their intake to so few cigarettes? Through sheer fear or discipline! Some are terrified to increase their intake, some can't afford to and others are ashamed to admit to being smokers, now that smoking is widely regarded as antisocial. Never forget:

1 No smoker actually chooses to become a smoker.

2 All smokers hate the thought of their parents, children or grandchildren falling into the trap.

3 No matter how honest they are in other ways, all drug addicts are liars about their own addiction. If only all smokers would tell the truth, we'd achieve our goal in no time!

THERE'S NO SUCH THING AS A 'HAPPY SMOKER'!

We've already shattered many important illusions. It's now time to move on to even more serious ones:

SMOKING RELIEVES BOREDOM

CHAPTER 17

ILLUSION – SMOKING
RELIEVES BOREDOM

If I were to market a pill that I claimed had the complete opposite effect to an identical pill from the same bottle taken an hour earlier, I'm convinced it wouldn't be long before I was accused of being a charlatan. Incredibly, society in general, and smokers in particular, have been making similar claims for generations. They claim that smoking relieves boredom and aids concentration – two diametrically opposed situations. They also claim smoking assists in both relaxing and stressful situations. Again – two diametrically opposed situations.

Such is the power of the brainwashing, reinforced by subsequent addiction to nicotine that billions of smokers have lived and died without even noticing this anomaly. In fact, I was the first to notice it when the blinkers dropped from my eyes on 15 July 1983. Amazingly, the only people who seem to be aware of it more than twenty years later are people who have sought help at one of my clinics, read one of my books or watched my DVD.

There is no doubt that smokers tend to smoke more when they are bored. But this doesn't mean that smoking relieves boredom. Of the hundreds of thousands of cigarettes I've smoked in my life, I cannot once remember thinking:

'I'm bored! What can I do to relieve the boredom? I know! I'll smoke a cigarette! I take the cigarette out of the packet, carefully place the tip end in my mouth, light up and then inhale the smoke. Then, I alternately exhale and inhale until I've finished the cigarette. Goodness, this is fascinating! If I'm still bored I can smoke another and another and another...'

What is so mind-absorbing about smoking a cigarette? As I've already explained, the vast majority of cigarettes are smoked mindlessly. I can hardly imagine a more boring pastime than chain smoking sixty to a hundred cigarettes a day for a third of a century!

If you have something to occupy your mind that isn't stressful, it tends to distract you from the 'little monster'. The reason smokers tend to smoke more when they are bored is because they have nothing to take their mind off the 'little monster'. In truth, smoking is a major cause of boredom. It drains your energy and your finances and leaves you feeling lethargic.

Next time you see a motorist stuck in rush hour traffic, or a long distance lorry driver lined up at Dover, or a nightwatchman, they may or may not be smoking, but one thing's for sure:

THEY WILL BE BORED

IN NO WAY DOES SMOKING RELIEVE BOREDOM

Now let's explode the myth that kept me hooked for a third of a century:

SMOKING ASSISTS CONCENTRATION

CHAPTER 18

ILLUSION – SMOKING ASSISTS CONCENTRATION

I had reached the stage in my decline into the smoking abyss where I had come to the conclusion that it was only the inability to concentrate without a cigarette that prevented me stopping. I could put up with the bad temper and misery; in fact I used to get a masochistic pleasure from the feeling of martyrdom.

My undoing was my job. I earned a relatively high salary for using my brain, but without cigarettes my brain was about as effective as a blob of putty. On a previous occasion, I had toyed with the idea of asking my boss if he would excuse me from any concentrated work for about a month. But he was a non-smoker and I knew he wouldn't understand, so I decided to arrange it for myself.

However, there was one ten-minute job I could neither delegate nor put off. It was the preparation of the monthly payroll. For the whole month, I played noughts and crosses with myself, whatever. At odd times, I would attempt to do the payroll, but each time the brain would switch off and I would leave it until the next day, until I could delay no longer. On the fatal day, I sat gazing at the payroll for two hours in a cold sweat. It was ridiculous.

I sneaked out, bought ten cigarettes, returned and completed the job in eight minutes flat! That incident proved to my satisfaction that I was unable to concentrate without smoking. Exactly *why* I couldn't I didn't know, any more than I knew why I scratched an itch.

There was another explanation. However, my ingenious, addicted, subconscious brain didn't want to know about it. Perhaps it had worked out that if I could suffer the misery of abstaining for a month – providing I didn't complete that ten-minute job – I would be able to say, with an absolutely clear conscience, to my family and myself: *'Bad luck old chap. It's not really your fault. It's just that you cannot function without cigarettes.'*

Obviously I didn't start the attempt in that frame of mind. Like all smokers who make a genuine attempt to stop by using the willpower method, I hoped that time would solve the problem. It didn't. The craving got worse as each day went by. But that ten-minute job was my lifeline. Had I completed it, I would have had no excuse to give in without ignominy.

Whether I believed I was genuinely incapable of concentrating without smoking at that time, I cannot tell. It doesn't really matter one way or another. The point was that I was miserable without the cigarettes and believed I always would be. That misconception was the true reason that I bought those cigarettes, but lack of concentration seemed a good scapegoat.

So, how can we prove whether smoking helps concentration or not? It is absolutely vital to do so because if you have the slightest doubt about it that doubt will guarantee you cannot concentrate without smoking.

There are clues to help us decide. One was another incident involving smoking and concentration. After three years of studying to be an accountant, I had to sit the intermediate examination. My employers generously granted me six weeks' study leave. After three weeks I learned that it was forbidden to smoke during the exam. Can you imagine my fury? I was already a chain smoker and the times when cigarettes were absolutely essential were the times I needed to concentrate. No way could I pass those exams without smoking. I had just found out that I'd spent three years studying subjects I loathed and was doomed to fail, all because some idiot had neglected to inform me at the start that you can't smoke during the exam.

I began to consider alternative employment. However, I'm not the type to surrender easily. Maybe it was possible to go three hours without a cigarette. I got a copy of examination questions from a previous year; set an alarm clock; tried to reproduce in my mind the tension of the actual exam; and succeeded so well that I couldn't stop my hand shaking sufficiently even to write, let alone think! Surely, it was absolute proof that you cannot concentrate without cigarettes?

That incident, now more than a third of a century ago, will forever remain vivid in my memory. Curious then, that I have no recollection whatsoever of another incident that happened shortly afterwards, which proved my conclusion wrong. The significance of this incident didn't occur to me until I had successfully quit smoking. I not only passed those exams but, whilst writing them, the thought of smoking never entered my head. Not even when it came to the crunch; not even when I was hopelessly addicted to nicotine and during what must have been one of the most tense, most stressful and highly concentrated three hours of my life:

I *DIDN'T* NEED THEM! IT WAS PURELY PSYCHOLOGICAL!

Now let us go back to the ten-minute job I couldn't complete without smoking. There was nothing complicated about it; it was purely routine. The only reason I hadn't delegated it was not due to its complexity but because of its confidential nature. I am not denying I couldn't concentrate without the cigarette at that time, but that was because I *genuinely believed* cigarettes helped me to concentrate. If you believe that, then it's impossible to concentrate without them.

Let us forget smoking for a moment and consider concentration. In order to concentrate, you first remove distractions. The children are making a noise, you can't concentrate. You have the choice of moving to another room or of yelling: *'Could you please keep the noise down, I'm trying to concentrate!'* It is within your power to remove the distraction and if you don't do so you will get uptight and irritable. Now, imagine you have a bad cold. You have to blow your nose every minute, which also makes it difficult for you to concentrate. But can you ever remember thinking: *'When will this cold go so that I can concentrate properly?'*

The difference is that if there is something that you can do to remove a distraction, you are distracted and irritable until you have removed it. If there is nothing you can do about it, you accept it and get on with it. A concert pianist will be distracted by the drop of a pin yet stock-brokers, commodity brokers and currency brokers are able to apply intense concentration during an atmosphere of sonic chaos. Has one ever suddenly shouted out:

'WILL YOU ALL JUST SHUT UP, I'M TRYING TO CONCENTRATE!'

So why the difference? Just this: a concert pianist expects perfect silence and will be distracted by anything less. The broker expects, and has no choice but to accept, sonic chaos. The non-smoker expects and accepts having mental blocks from time to time. And what do they do when they have mental blocks? They either take a break and hope that solves their problem or they just get on with it. What do smokers do when they have mental blocks? They light a cigarette. The probability is that they were already smoking when those mental blocks arose; people in professions that depend on concentration or inspiration tend to chain smoke at such times. I admit that many smokers find it impossible to concentrate without smoking, but that's only because they have the permanent 'itch' and their inability to scratch it will distract them from the problem of their mental block. In fact, it will supersede that problem. Why else do smokers drive around in the small hours searching for an all-night garage? When someone is a smoker with a mental block, can they honestly say that the moment they light a cigarette the block mysteriously evaporates? If so, it would mean smokers never suffer from mental blocks. That is obviously nonsense. So how do smokers overcome mental blocks? In exactly the same way non-smokers do:

THEY JOLLY WELL GET ON WITH IT!

What is certain is that when I extinguished my final cigarette, I was neither aware of being unable to concentrate nor of any other unpleasant symptoms I had suffered on previous attempts. So, why do smokers often suffer a lack of concentration when they attempt to stop?

Some believe it is due to the actual physical withdrawal from nicotine, but that is so slight it's imperceptible. The real problem is that the ex-smoker's brain has been programmed to believe that when they get a mental block there is a simple solution. Obviously, for a few days after the final cigarette, the 'little monster' will be nagging away; and for a while, whenever they have a mental block, it triggers the thought: *'Have a cigarette.'* This is the crunch. You are taken unawares. The natural tendency is to think: *'At times like this I would have lit a cigarette, now what have I got?'* Yes, you would have lit a cigarette, but it wouldn't have done the slightest good.

The problem is that you are no longer even trying to solve the problem of the mental block. You are thinking about smoking and while you're doing that, you'll obviously be unable to concentrate on anything else. That loss of concentration, in turn, causes you to question whether smoking does, in fact, aid concentration. Doubt creeps in and you begin to feel deprived. Now you will be thinking: *'Perhaps I should try one cigarette, just to test it out.'* If you do light one you no longer have to go through the thought process of: *'Should I or shouldn't I?'* Now all that remains is to get on with solving the mental block and since your brain isn't being distracted by whether or not you should smoke, in all probability you solve your problem and so perpetuate the illusion that smoking helps concentration. On the other hand, if you hadn't lit that cigarette the doubt would have continued in your mind, thus guaranteeing that:

YOU WON'T BE ABLE TO CONCENTRATE!

Why is it that, from whichever angle you look at it, the cigarette always seems to end up the winner? It's because it's an incredibly ingenious trap. But I remind you that provided you understand it, it's easy to quit. So how do we avoid these triggers, not only for those few days after the final cigarette, but for the rest of our lives? You cannot avoid them. Even to attempt to avoid them is to court disaster and misery. Remember, Easyway is about changing one's frame of mind. Why was it that during the trial run for that exam, I couldn't even write, let alone concentrate? Yet, during the actual exam, the lack of cigarettes didn't bother me in spite of the fact I believed I was completely and utterly dependent on cigarettes? It was because I had no doubt. I *knew* I couldn't smoke.

I said I never even thought about smoking during that exam. Perhaps I did at odd times and just don't remember. If so, the reason I don't remember was because I didn't waste further time dwelling on it. I knew I couldn't smoke, so I got on with the matter in hand. Perhaps you're thinking: *'You didn't have to use any willpower because you had no choice, but what about the poor ex-smokers who haven't got anyone to force them to stop?'*

It wasn't the forcing that did it. We've already established that the more you try to force smokers to stop, the greater will be their resistance. It was:

CERTAINTY THAT WAS THE KEY!
THE LACK OF DOUBT!

That's another thing Easyway does, it prepares smokers, so that if or when these triggers come:

THEY NEVER DOUBT

Far from assisting concentration, smoking perpetually and increasingly starves every muscle and organ of oxygen and nutrients, gunging them up with carbon monoxide and other poisons, which seriously impedes the normal functioning of the brain. Furthermore, the mere activity of smoking is a distraction. There are no genuine advantages to smoking.

Removing the illusion that smoking aids concentration is vital. Now we're about to remove one of the biggest illusions of all:

SMOKING HELPS YOU RELAX

CHAPTER 19

ILLUSION– SMOKING HELPS YOU RELAX

Jenny is a traffic warden, a nice one – fair-minded and pleasant. She even gives you the ticket with a nice smile. It's a Friday evening and London's in the middle of its worst heat wave for five years. She's just finished her final shift of the week. Her feet are killing her and, still an hour from home, she's already anticipating the removal of those shoes.

Jenny is also a smoker who is trying to cut down. She smoked her last cigarette during her mid-afternoon break and is now looking forward to her favourite cigarette: the one when she's safely reached the comfort of her flat. Luck is on her side. A bus arrives just as she reaches the stop and she is the last to board. She has no luck with a seat however. She blames that on the uniform and doesn't mind, as she is rapidly being taken home.

The moment she enters the flat she kicks off her shoes and the relief is immense. It crosses her mind to smoke the cigarette there and then, but Jenny is a disciplined person and decides to wait for the perfect moment. She switches on the TV to catch the news and quenches her thirst with a nice cup of tea.

Then, she luxuriates in the bath for twenty minutes while she cleanses her body of London's grime and, finally, cooks a ready-prepared meal in the microwave. Having disposed of the wrapping, she places her meal on a tray, pours herself a glass of her favourite wine and watches the latest edition of her favourite soap opera. After the meal she smokes that precious cigarette. *'Absolute bliss,'* she thinks.

Now, in case you think I'm promoting the joys of smoking, let me remind you that my sole purpose at this moment is to prove to you that in no way does smoking help you to relax. Let's analyze what actually happened. The first thing Jenny did when she entered the flat was to remove her uncomfortable shoes. No doubt she let out a sigh of relief as she did so. Did this action confer any other advantages? For example, did it:

a Quench her thirst?
b Remove the grime from her body?
c Satisfy her hunger?
d Relieve her boredom?

The answer is clear and obvious in each case: **No!** The purpose of the action was to remove just one slight aggravation. It is equally obvious that each other action was also designed to remove another slight aggravation. Did the cigarette quench her thirst, remove the grime from her body, satisfy her hunger or relieve her boredom? Obviously not! It too was designed to fulfil just one function and one function alone:

TO SATISFY THE INSATIABLE APPETITE OF THE 'LITTLE MONSTER'

WHICH IT CAN NEVER DO!

Now, please re-read the above story and see each action as removing some minor stress. That's what complete relaxation amounts to:

REMOVAL OF STRESS

Every action Jenny took aided relaxation by relieving stress, with one notable exception:

SMOKING IMPEDES RELAXATION AND CAUSES STRESS

The only stress a cigarette can relieve is the stress of the body withdrawing from nicotine, the 'little monster', plus any additional mental aggravation caused by not being allowed to relieve it immediately. When Jenny first entered her flat, it crossed her mind to light up immediately. She had to discipline herself not to do so, thus taming the 'big monster'. When she finally allowed herself to satisfy the aggravation, it would have appeared like absolute bliss to her, because that was the final aggravation she removed. That cigarette made the difference between being stressed and completely relaxed and that's why it appeared so precious to her.

Of course, in reality, the only aggravation that the cigarette relieved was that caused by nicotine withdrawal from the cigarette she smoked during her mid-afternoon break.

Because the relief was only partial, and because all that has happened is that the dose of nicotine has staved off the need for another cigarette for a brief few minutes, she has actually perpetuated the aggravation rather than relieved it. After all, non-smokers don't get uptight after meals, with drinks or at social occasions when smoking isn't allowed. Smoking causes the very stress that smokers believe it relieves.

The final illusion I need to shatter is that:

'A CIGARETTE IS MY FRIEND, MY COMFORT, MY COMPANION'

CHAPTER 20

ILLUSION – A CIGARETTE IS MY FRIEND, MY COMFORT, MY COMPANION

I'm told that the advertising campaign for Strand cigarettes was a failure. However, the slogan:

'YOU'RE NEVER ALONE WITH A STRAND'

certainly summed up my feelings towards cigarettes. Provided I had a packet of cigarettes in my pocket I didn't need any other companion. I felt strong and secure, able to stand up to whatever life threw at me.

The reality was the complete opposite. I reached the stage where I couldn't change a TV programme without first lighting up a cigarette. Even with hindsight, it's difficult for me to imagine the damage I was inflicting on my body and the damage I was doing to my courage and confidence was even more devastating.

I am not a member of any established church and I don't pretend to understand the power that helped release me from the nicotine trap. All I know is that somebody up there was looking after me and has done ever since. It was like awakening from a nightmare black and white world of fear and depression, into a colourful world of strength and happiness. More than twenty years later, I still cannot get over the joy of being free. Having woken from that nightmare, I find it inconceivable that the drug I now see as Devastation was once regarded as a friend, comfort and companion. Such is the power of the brainwashing.

We have now shattered all the illusions about how smoking provides some form of pleasure or crutch and we are left with justifications like: *'I enjoy smoking'* or *'I just love the ritual'*. Ask smokers to explain what is so enjoyable about paying through the nose for the privilege of inhaling filthy cancerous fumes into their lungs and they'll be at a loss to do so. The only reason we believe we enjoy smoking is because when we try to quit by using willpower we are miserable and assume we wouldn't smoke if we didn't enjoy it.

Let's compare the ritual of smoking with the ritual of a meal. For many years, most Saturday nights you have dined out with your partner and a couple who are your best friends. You are particularly looking forward to this Saturday because it's your birthday. It's Norman's turn to pay and he's booked the best table at the poshest restaurant in town.

You receive a cordial welcome from the owner who, with a nod from Norman, serves champagne. Eventually, you are escorted to your table, which is a delight to behold. The linen, the silver, the flowers, the crockery, the crystal and the background music are all perfection.

As you slowly browse through the menu, irresistible aromas are wafting through from the kitchen and you start to feel hungry but you're in no hurry.

Eventually, you order and an hour later your favourite starter is placed in front of you. No sooner has it arrived than it's whipped away, never to return. Norman then explains how you had assured him that the most important aspect of a meal was not the food, but the company, the atmosphere and the service in that order.

Obviously the above scenario would never arise, but imagine it did. Do you think you would be a happy bunny? I love the ritual of eating out, but the whole object of that ritual is to satisfy hunger. Unless you do that, it's pointless.

The whole object of the smoking ritual is to satisfy your craving for nicotine. This is why you'll never learn to enjoy herbal cigarettes – they contain no nicotine! More confirmation of what I've been saying all along:

SMOKING IS NOTHING MORE OR LESS THAN ADDICTION TO NICOTINE

We now turn again to a ruse which has been successfully used by the pharmaceutical industry to pressurize governments and the medical establishment, to endorse the absurd practice of prescribing nicotine to cure nicotine addiction, so-called:

CLINICAL TRIALS AND SUCCESS RATES

CHAPTER 21

CLINICAL TRIALS AND SUCCESS RATES

Imagine you are an Olympic athletics coach. A close friend phones you, in some excitement, with news of a really bright prospect and invites you to take the youngster under your wing. His name is Bob and his preferred event is the 100 metres. You enquire about his best time and are told that he has yet to complete the course. Obviously, you are somewhat confused. Even so, you agree to meet him at your local athletics ground in order to check him out.

Bob arrives and you are delighted to observe that he has the ideal build for a sprinter. You then invite him to run the 100 metres track. He walks to the start line and, to your astonishment, ties his ankles together with a piece of rope and places a hood over his head. He then tries to run but only succeeds in falling flat on his face.

You are now convinced you are the butt of some bizarre joke. You remove the hood, untie his ankles and start to question him. Bob explains that up to now he's had three separate coaches, each of whom has advised him that if ever he wants to be a great sprinter, the rope and the hood are essential. True, it will take immense willpower but there are no shortcuts.

You've been coaching athletes for years but wouldn't need any of your vast experience to know Bob will do much better without the rope and the hood. However, being a cautious man you check it out with the head of your coaches association who informs you they have a national policy based on the method of Bob's previous three coaches.

Do you believe such a bizarre situation could actually arise? By now you are probably convinced I'm the joker. In fact, this situation has existed for more than twenty years and we're not just talking about a few athletes being tripped up, but more than 100,000 British smokers who die from smoking annually and the millions who continue their addiction to nicotine being kept in ignorance of an immediate, easy and permanent cure. Moreover, a similar number of youngsters, had they been informed of the facts, could have been prevented from falling into the trap. Bear in mind I don't produce these statistics; they come from the same Government and medical profession whose policies are failing year after year.

The attitude of 'the Big 3' has been and still is: *'Try this method, if that doesn't work, try that.'* Supposing they applied the same philosophy to all diseases and actually recommended a treatment that kills 90 per cent of patients whilst ignoring one that cures 90 per cent? I strongly urge the Government and medical profession to take responsibility for their actions. Surely they run the risk of incurring truly enormous damages as a result of such negligence.

Perhaps you believe the analogy I've used is ridiculous and grossly exaggerated. After all, it doesn't take an Olympic coach to know that tying an athlete's feet together and placing a hood over his head, far from improving his performance, is going to have the completely opposite effect.

It's blatantly obvious. But whilst **'the Big 3'** and smokers themselves, concentrate their efforts on why people shouldn't smoke and why smoking bans are necessary, they miss the real problem, which is to remove the reasons that keep people hooked.

Once you understand the nicotine trap, all myths and illusions are shattered in an instant and it becomes obvious that to use any method other than Easyway makes about as much sense as using the rope and hood to run well – and you don't need unscientific and inaccurate trials to prove it.

ALL YOU NEED IS PLAIN COMMON SENSE!

Our Director of Business Development, John Dicey, dedicated huge efforts to what proved to be an abortive attempt to persuade the National Institute for Health and Clinical Excellence (NICE) to evaluate Easyway.

NICE is the body that recommends that NHS clinics advocate NRT. John was curious to know what success rates the NRT advocates were claiming and how accessible the facts were to a smoker considering their options, before an attempt to quit. The following is a synopsis of his activities, commenced on 15 October 2002.

A TV production company had requested that he research the effectiveness of Easyway compared to NRT and the smoking-cessation drug, Zyban, in time to discuss a Channel 4 documentary on the stunning success of the Allen Carr method of smoking cessation.

John started with the ASH website, which proved to be inconclusive. So he telephoned them, masquerading as a smoker wanting information on success rates so he could choose the best option. They suggested he ring the NHS Smoking Helpline. They recommended NRT straight away. He enquired about the success rate and was told:

'It's different for different people . . . depends how much you want to stop.'

John pointed out that if they were recommending it to people, surely they should have some idea of the success rate. He was then asked to call back to talk to a senior counsellor.

He phoned back later and spoke to Debbie, who was also reluctant to discuss success rates. When pushed, she said it was around 50 per cent but that was just her best guess, and went on to explain that it was different for different people.

John asked her to check with someone who would know. She called back suggesting that he call ASH. Circuit complete! Instead, he asked her for the names of the NRT manufacturers and was informed that she wasn't allowed to divulge that information.

John then phoned Quitline, again under the pretence of being a would-be quitter. QUIT is partly funded by the NRT and Zyban manufacturers and John was informed they recommended both products and that both had: '*Very high success rates.*' He asked what the success rate was:

'*Um, don't quote me on this, but it's about 25 to 30 per cent . . . I think. It's a while since I trained, but I'm sure that's what they told me.*'

Again he asked her to consult someone who would know. You've guessed it; she suggested that he contact ASH. Circuit two complete.

Undaunted, John decided to ask about three different brands of nicotine patches at separate pharmacies. None of the pharmacists knew the success rate other than: '*They double your chances of success!*' I thought the Advertising Standards Authority (ASA) was supposed to have ruled out misleading adverts. That phrase can mean a success rate of anything from zero to 100 per cent. Do you see what I mean about statistics?

Not to be beaten, and having purchased a variety of nicotine patches for reference, John decided to contact the manufacturers/suppliers, again posing as a would-be quitter:

Nicotinell

Incredibly, the only telephone number given with this product was Quitline, who didn't know the success rate.

John then phoned the Consumer Health Department at the manufacturers, Novartis. He was told: *'Using NRT means you are twice as likely to quit!'* John said he'd heard the success rate was about 2 per cent using willpower alone and suggested that if that was the case, the success rate of their product would be about 4 per cent. The Novartis man paused and said he thought willpower would be more like 5 per cent. Strange that he should purport to know more about the willpower method than his own product.

John said:

'So with NRT it's about a 10 per cent success rate?'

The reply was:

'Oh yes, although it does improve if you can get support from your GP or an NHS clinic. I have seen some research that seems to suggest this, but there is not a lot of evidence to support it.'

Surprise, surprise.

Nicorette

Apart from Quitline's telephone number (which had already proved to be a dead end), the pack contained a 'Fresh Start' number, which John tried. He was informed there had been several studies and that the one this person had in front of her was a double-blind placebo study that shows a success rate of 18 to 77 per cent, compared to a 3 to 39 per cent success rate when a placebo was used. Don't even bother trying to make sense of that.

John asked:

'So what is the overall success rate for the majority of users? 17 per cent to 77 per cent is a massive variation!'

'Um . . . well it does depend on how much the smoker wants to stop, and how much or how long they've smoked for.'

'So you don't have an overall, average success rate?'

'No, it just depends!'

'What does it depend on?'

'It just depends.'

Thankfully, John ended the conversation there. However, he persevered with the third manufacturer:

NiQuitin

John phoned but couldn't get an immediate answer to his question. He was phoned back after two hours by Amy, who had to go on the internet to find some studies, all conducted by the pharmaceutical companies. She quoted a success rate of 26 per cent after about six months.

Meanwhile, partly to pass the time, John phoned Nicotinell again and pointed out that Nicorette claimed a success rate of between 17 to 77 per cent and asked why Nicotinell was only 10 per cent? I quote their reply:

'I see. Nicorette have been in a lot of trouble because of some of the things they've been saying, claims they've been making. They've been fined. The Cochrane group is an independent body that assesses things for the Government, and they say that there is no difference between success rates of all brands of patches. The success rate they are quoting must be from their own research, rather than research accepted by the Government. How can I put this without getting into legal trouble . . . ?'

The following important factors must be blatantly obvious from the above:

Either the Government, the NHS, NICE and/or the pharmaceutical companies have completed effective clinical studies or they haven't. If they have, why is it so difficult for those interested in using the products to ascertain their chances of success? Why all the doubt and secrecy?

CHAPTER 22

WELCOME TO THE MEDICINES BUSINESS

The medicines business is by no means straightforward. Clinical studies have been done into smoking cessation methods but the vast majority – certainly those that are widely publicized – are paid for by the pharmaceutical companies that manufacture the products. They pay doctors to conduct the trials and they say what questions are to be asked, what constitutes success and so on. Then they use the billions of promotional dollars they have at their disposal to publicize the results that suit them best.

Most ordinary people find it hard just to imagine what a billion dollars looks like, let alone what it can buy. Dr Marcia Angell, a former editor of the esteemed *New England Journal of Medicine*, did her best to educate the public when she wrote her book *The Truth About the Drug Companies: How They Deceive Us and What to Do About It.*[13]

She carved up the income from these massive companies as follows: research and development of new drugs took the smallest share (14 per cent); around 17 per cent went in profits; the largest share went on marketing and administration, which took as much as the first two again (31 per cent). The rest went on things like manufacturing, distribution and so on. In 2005, drugs companies earned $600 billion, just under half of which came from the US on its own. That means, if my mathematics serves me correctly, that companies had around $186 billion or £98 billion that year to spend on marketing and administration, more than half of which is spent in the freest medicine market in the world.

Most of this money goes on marketing. What on earth does all this money buy? Before considering that important question, it is worth putting the amounts of money into a bit more perspective. Henry A. Waxman, a Californian Democrat, did this when he wrote in the *New England Journal of Medicine*:

'The pharmaceutical industry spends more than $5.5 billion to promote drugs to doctors [in the US] each year – more than what all US medical schools spend to educate medical students.' [14]

More money being spent on promoting drugs to doctors than in educating them to appreciate their value goes a long way to explaining my frustration at the conference in Beijing, where I was invited to talk, but no one wanted to listen. Dr Richard Horton, editor of the UK medical journal, the *Lancet,* goes even further. He describes pharmaceutical marketing missions as information laundering operations. Here's how it works:

'*A pharmaceutical company will sponsor a scientific meeting. Speakers will be invited to talk about a product, and they will be paid a hefty fee (several thousand pounds) for doing so. A pharmaceutical communications company will record this lecture and convert it into an article for publication, usually as part of a collection of papers emanating from the symposium. This collection will be offered to a medical publisher for an amount that can run into hundreds of thousands of pounds. The publisher will then seek a reputable journal to publish the papers based on the symposium.*' [15]

The important point, he stresses, is that the process by which science is verified by other scientists knowledgeable in the field hardly exists. This is known as 'peer review' and is important because it is supposed to ensure there is no bias or distortion in the results. Horton continues:

'*The process of publication has been reduced to marketing dressed up as legitimate science. Pharmaceutical companies have found a way to circumvent the protective norms of peer review. In all too many cases, they are able to seed the research literature with weak science that they can then use to promote their products to physicians.*' [16]

Jacky Law's book *Big Pharma*, completes the picture:

'*That science filters down the knowledge chain, being interpreted at every juncture by people with no reason to question pharma's findings. Drug company money effectively pays the wages of everyone writing for healthcare professionals because it buys the ads that make their publications viable. The reporting of clinical trials and scientific conferences is coloured at every turn by the general understanding that it is not a good idea to bite the hand that feeds you. Anything untoward about these powerful patrons gets scant coverage because that isn't how the system works . . .*

Pharma companies, working through third parties, have been able to influence, if not control, every salient aspect of the healthcare agenda for years, whether it is how drugs are researched or how those results are made known.' [17]

Clearly, one cannot rely on pharmaceutical companies to run fair and open clinical trials. Indeed, if you have any doubts, two events that happened in 2004 should remove them. One was the worldwide withdrawal of the popular painkiller Vioxx that quickly became the subject of lawsuits around the world.

Vioxx was a drug that had been shown in 2000 to significantly increase the risk of a heart attack. Despite this evidence, the drug was able to continue earning $2.5 billion a year worldwide for a further four years. The head of cardiovascular medicine at the respected Cleveland Clinic in Ohio, Dr Eric Topol, tried repeatedly to publicize the risks during this time but suffered relentless attacks on his personal and professional life:

'You are putting yourself at risk when you speak out in the public interest,' he said in Law's book Big Pharma.

'The resources open to the industry are extraordinary and you find yourself in a very nasty and imperiled situation. It shouldn't be this way but it is.'[18]

That same year, 2004, the safety profile of the equally popular antidepressant Seroxat was rewritten. This was the subject of a BBC *Panorama* programme that prompted such an avalanche of response from the public that the chief medicines regulator in the UK, Professor Alasdair Breckenridge, was forced to answer questions on national television as to why they hadn't been better protected. No fewer than 1,370 people had responded to the programme with horrendous accounts of their experiences on the drug or, more usually, when they tried to come off it. The most stunning aspect of the programme was that these people had tried to tell their doctors and the authorities about the side-effects of this popular drug. But no one was listening.

The unsolicited reports that viewers had emailed into the *Panorama* team were analyzed and published in the *International Journal of Risk & Safety in Medicine*. In all, there were 16 suicides, 47 cases of attempted suicide, 92 people who had thoughts of harming themselves or others and 19 children who had suffered serious side-effects. One doctor, Professor David Healy, summed up the sorry episode well at the UK inquiry into the industry:

'Here in the UK, we track the fate of parcels through the post 100 times more accurately than you [the regulators] track the fate of people who have been killed by drugs.'[19]

If you think this has no relevance to smoking, think again. In New York, at around the same time, the makers of Seroxat – or Paxil as it is known in the US – were being challenged by the Attorney General, Eliot Spitzer. Spitzer wasn't a scientist or a doctor. He was simply concerned as a human being – as I am – about the claims drugs companies can make about their products by concealing studies that don't show good results.

Spitzer accused UK drugs giant GlaxoSmithKline of *'repeated and persistent fraud'* for concealing vital safety information when this particular drug is used in children. He pointed out that the company had done several studies, only one of which generated the results it wanted. In one study that was not published, for example, it was found that 7.7 per cent of the young people taking the drug had suicidal thoughts, compared with just 3 per cent of the placebo arm.[20] The drugs company chose to settle the affair with a one-off $250 million fine and an agreement to set up a public register of all clinical trials on all of its drugs.

SEARCHING FOR THE TRUTH

The events of 2004 were something of a watershed for the industry. But having one company agree to make its clinical trials public was a small victory. The odds in the wider information war are still overwhelmingly on the side of the giant companies. Clinical studies that show NRT doesn't work are now coming to light.

One, published in the April 2005 edition of *Addiction*, showed the success rates of a one-year UK programme, pitting the various quitting methods against each other. This showed that more than a quarter (25.5 per cent) of cold turkey quitters were still not smoking, compared with only 15.2 per cent of NRT quitters, 14.4 per cent of Zyban users and 7.4 per cent of people who were using both NRT and Zyban.

It is almost farcical. The people who take Zyban and NRT do worst of all by far. I wouldn't be at all surprised if they were also secretly puffing on cigarettes as well, poisoning their systems with an abundance of nicotine that is paid for by the NHS, at prices that are comparable with what is charged for cigarettes.

The irony of it all is that the price of cigarettes reflects the high taxation that is levied because smoking is a lethal *habit*. Successive chancellors have been able to increase the price of a pack of cigarettes because, being such a dangerous *habit*, they know no one will object. But then, in an extraordinary twist of logic, the NHS uses taxpayers' money to pay similar prices for NRT products so people can continue to poison themselves for free, while also maintaining their addiction to nicotine.

As it happens, the NHS has negotiated itself some discounts. The price of seven 15 mg Nicorette patches, for example, is £15.99 if you buy them at a high street chemist, compared with an NHS purchase price of £9.07 – a reduction of around 43 per cent. But there are no patents on nicotine or any of the most common ways of delivering nicotine into the body. There is no reason why Nicorette gum should cost more than Wrigley's Spearmint, for example; other than the more stringent manufacturing requirements you get with medicines and, of course, the fact that companies can get away with it. As the price of cigarettes goes up, what the Treasury gains in taxes goes straight to the pharmaceutical industry via the NHS.

How can taxpayers and smokers be conned in this way?

CHAPTER 23

THE ECONOMICS

One reason taxpayers and smokers can be conned in the way explained in the previous chapter is impressive statistical footwork. Let me give you the figures from a series of articles published in the *British Medical Journal*. The series was called 'ABC of Smoking Cessation', and was edited by Professor John Britton of City Hospital, Nottingham, who admits to having been paid by GlaxoSmithKline for attending two international conferences, and by Pharmacia (owned by Pfizer) for being the lead investigator in a clinical trial of NRT.

The figures quoted in the series are impressive. In the UK, the treatment of smoking-related diseases has been estimated to cost the NHS £1.4 billion to £1.5 billion a year. [21] As you can see, there are lots of savings to be made. Easyway can make these savings without costing the NHS a penny – but that is not taken on board by the people who make the decisions on behalf of the public.

The first thing to grasp is that all the calculations that are made are based on initial assumptions that NRT and Zyban do some good – which I think I have shown by now is highly questionable. NICE, which works out if treatments represent value for money for the NHS, uses studies done by drugs companies to calculate the number of years of life that might be saved by particular drugs. Then, based on the assumption that an NHS life is worth around £30,000 a year, it arrives at a figure to show how much these drugs cost to save a year of life.

NICE estimates that it costs the NHS between £1,000 and £2,400 per life-year saved if NRT and advice are provided. Zyban represents a rather better deal, costing from £645 to £1,500 per life-year saved. If advice, NRT and Zyban are all provided by the NHS, the cost per life-year saved is between £890 and £1,970. [21] You don't have to be an expert to know that if the initial figures are distorted, so are the ones that come out at the other end. Nor do you have to be a health economist to realize that if the NHS funds treatments that cost up to £30,000 for every life-year gained, then these figures do represent value for money *in the minds of the people at NICE.*

At this stage I should point out that Easyway has made several well-resourced attempts to engage with NICE in a professional, strategic manner over the past 36 months. NICE have refused to even evaluate the method. But that didn't stop them enquiring about our corporate service, with a view to us helping their staff quit smoking. Strange they would even consider such a thing, given their decision to bar our method but make NRT and Zyban available to the public via the NHS.

Even when a decision was made to let private companies – like my own – apply to run NHS stop smoking clinics, Easyway has met with brick wall after brick wall to even be considered as a contender. Dubious figures from dubious sources purport to show NRT products and Zyban providing value for money. Everyone is missing the simple truth that *nicotine* is the evil poison that people are addicted to. Changing the delivery system of getting the drug into the body from cigarettes to patches, inhalers or chewing gum, may be convenient for people who don't want to be antisocial and it may seem helpful to people who can't afford to pay for cigarettes but can get their nicotine at the taxpayer's expense,

BUT IT DOESN'T CHANGE THE FACT THAT KEEPING PEOPLE ADDICTED TO NICOTINE LIKE THIS HELPS NO ONE BUT THE DRUGS COMPANIES.

What about the doctors?

If this really is the case, why don't doctors speak up? Aren't they on our side? The truth is that half the time they are almost as much in the dark as Joe Bloggs. Family doctors around the world continued to prescribe Vioxx for four years, for example, not realizing it was positively dangerous for anyone with a weak heart. Indeed, in every major scandal involving the drug industry, GPs have been the last to know the real risks and benefits associated with drugs.

How can doctors know the unvarnished truth when so many billions of pounds are tied up promoting their benefits and downplaying their risks? As we have seen, more money is spent in the US promoting drugs to doctors than is spent by all the medical schools combined in educating them. In the UK, the parliamentary inquiry into the industry's influence found the Department of Health spends around £4.5 million a year providing independent medicines information to prescribers. This, they said, represents about 0.3 per cent of the approximately £1.65 billion a year that the pharmaceutical industry spends promoting their drugs to doctors. [22]

This promotional money pays for vast armies of salesmen who do nothing other than visit doctors in their surgeries, take them out to lunch, and generally do whatever it takes to persuade them of the value of their products. Where smoking is concerned, this isn't difficult. Everyone knows smoking is bad. The Government has targets to get the numbers of smokers down. These reps offer help. What most family doctors don't know is how much the so-called Key Opinion Leaders, (known as KOLs), get paid to do the research that these reps use to promote their products. KOLs are specialist doctors paid by medical communications companies to promote drugs to other doctors through presentations, research papers, discussions and debates.

'The relationship between companies and KOLs is not explicitly transparent,' said a report from Consumers International, a federation of consumer organizations that looked into the marketing practices of twenty of the world's biggest drug companies in 2006. *'As a conse-*

quence, consumers and patients, and in some cases health professionals, may not always be aware how motivation for individual profit could play into the drug information they receive via the KOLs.'[23]

The report found that these twenty top drugs companies had been involved in no fewer than 972 breaches of the pharma industry's voluntary Code of Conduct between 2002 and 2005. And it should be mentioned that this code is voluntary. Drugs companies are policed, in other words, by their own trade association, the Association of the British Pharmaceutical Industry (ABPI). More than 35 per cent of these breaches – the largest category – had to do with misleading drug information. Many others were to do with offering free samples of drugs, kickbacks and gifts to doctors. The report's authors concluded:

'Consumers are in the dark about how their medicine consumption choices are the result of veiled relationships between doctors and the pharmaceutical companies. We believe that doctors should have their patients' interests as a priority rather than personal profit.'

In an article in the *Mail on Sunday*, 4 July 2004, Dr Desmond Spence had the guts to admit he had become the tool of the pharmaceutical industry. Other doctors have also had the courage to come clean. A GP who attended one of the annual conferences of our organization said that in around 80 per cent of cases he had no confidence the drug he was prescribing would bring any benefit to his patient.

He added that he thought this was typical of most GP practices.

When one considers that 50 to 80 per cent of the UK population don't take their medicines as instructed, it seems an awful lot of money is going straight into the pockets of the big pharma companies.

I salute the bravery of the doctors who do speak out and wish more would.

The pharmaceutical industry is also able to exert its pervasive influence over the media in ways which other commercial industries can only dream of. Allow me to relate my experience on:

THE *RICHARD & JUDY* SHOW

CHAPTER 24

THE *RICHARD & JUDY* SHOW

I was looking forward to appearing on Channel 4. I'd watched the show a couple of times and I thought they both had the easy, laid-back manner that would enable me to help some smokers to quit.

I was very nervous as I sat in the green room before the show. I always am in such situations. Being on a show like that is a wonderful opportunity to spread the good news, but time is always too short. It takes five hours at our clinics to convert a smoker into a happy non-smoker and on TV it's easy to waste the whole interview without making one positive contribution.

I sat next to my wife Joyce, quietly discussing the show. On my right sat a nervous-looking young lady from QUIT. Suddenly, a man appeared between us holding a cardboard box containing various nicotine products with the brand names clearly visible. He explained something to the lady from QUIT who looked just as flustered as I felt. The man then turned and informed me that I wasn't allowed to mention the name of my clinics and books on the show.

They had filmed a session at our London clinic the previous day; however, wherever our name was shown, it was concealed by an opaque visual effect. I asked him why I couldn't mention the name of my book or clinics – Allen Carr's Easyway – and he told me it was because I was a brand name. I don't know who this man was and presume he was connected with product marketing. There he was with a basket full of nicotine patches and gum, openly promoting the brand names of huge *pharmaceutical* companies. Moreover, during the interview the lady from QUIT was shown with the basket of NRT products, with the brand names clearly visible. At one point, a pack of Zyban was featured in close-up for a number of seconds. At the same time, I was told I couldn't even mention my own name!

At the actual interview I was introduced as Dr Carr from America. I took the form of address as a compliment and have nothing whatever against Americans or doctors, but I am neither. I happen to be proud to be British – and of my discovery – and I sincerely hope it is the British media that expose this scandal.

One of the troubles becoming increasingly obvious to me is that no one can see what is going on. And pharma's pervasive influence over the political process doesn't help. I am sure you will be as intrigued as I was to learn how patient interests are represented in Europe. Dr Andrew Herxheimer, Emeritus Fellow of the respected UK Cochrane Centre, explains in Jacky Law's book *Big Pharma*, how patient groups that are supposed to represent the public at the European level have in fact been established to support the aims of industry. [24]

The International Alliance of Patients' Organizations (IAPO), for example, is registered as a foundation in the Netherlands and funded by Pharmaceutical Partners for Better Healthcare – a consortium of about thirty major companies. And the Global Alliance of Mental Illness Advocacy Networks (GAMIAN) was founded by US pharma company Bristol-Myers Squibb, and has since developed its own autonomous European arm, GAMIAN-Europe.

'The European Commission prefers to hold discussions with these federations rather than patient and consumer groups, apparently because, unlike most voluntary health organizations, they claim to represent patients in many countries,' says Herxheimer. 'Neither publishes its source of funds.' [25]

Let's now take a closer look at:

WHY 'THE BIG 3' HAVE FAILED TO SOLVE THE DRUGS PROBLEM

CHAPTER 25

WHY 'THE BIG 3' HAVE FAILED TO SOLVE THE DRUGS PROBLEM

How can we rid society of this 21st-century equivalent of the Black Death? Up until now, we have failed even to check the expansion rate of drug addiction. To date there have been six main approaches to the problem:

1   Shock treatment
This involves massive publicity telling addicts what they already know: that it's killing them, costing them a fortune and that they are fools. Not only has this approach failed to cure most addicts, it doesn't even prevent non-addicts from getting hooked.

2   The search for suitable substitutes
For a smoker who is suffering the illusion that smoking provides them with a genuine pleasure or crutch, the ideal substitute would have, among others, the following properties:

a Be relaxing
b Relieve stress
c Assist concentration
d Relieve boredom

Since nicotine does none of these things, is anybody likely to find a substitute? And since nicotine is also:

 e The number one killer in Western society
 f Costs a fortune
 g Enslaves you for life
 h Is a filthy disgusting drug addiction

WHY ON EARTH WOULD ANYONE WANT A SUBSTITUTE?

3   Altering the social and environmental problems that make people turn to drugs

I'm all for doing that for its own sake, but alcohol, nicotine and heroin have proved there are no social or class barriers to drug addiction. To succeed, it would be necessary to remove all forms of stress from life. A nice thought, but not realistic.

4   The Narcotics Anonymous (NA) or Alcoholics Anonymous (AA) approach

While I have no wish to knock NA or AA, as I'm aware that many feel their lives have been saved by them, I consider their approach to be fundamentally flawed because it implies that the problem lies in the nature of the addict rather than the drugs themselves and society's attitude towards them. Hence, addicts are told they are suffering from an incurable disease and have to remain *in recovery* for the rest of their lives. The beautiful truth is Easyway provides a cure for drug addiction whereby the addict can break completely FREE.

5   Banning advertising

This has similar disadvantages to banning the drugs themselves. I know that in the countries in which advertising has been banned, statistics are produced to show that consumption of tobacco has gone down. I've already given my opinion on statistics and know just how misleading they can be, particularly where special interests are concerned, as is the case with both scientists and politicians. Consider this example: *'The rate of increase in inflation has gone down for the third month running.'* You might be excused for thinking that was good news, especially when announced in a tone that implies it *is*. It actually means inflation has gone up for the third month running! Going back to the figures following a ban on advertising tobacco, even if they were correct and not presented in a misleading manner, how do they know it is the ban on advertising that has caused the drop in consumption? After all, there has been a considerable drop in the use of tobacco in the UK in recent years, prior to the advertising ban.

6   Eradicating the supply of the drugs

This is the 'King Canute' approach. Every week we hear the authorities have busted a huge drugs ring and are winning the battle against the drug dealers

YET AT THE SAME TIME, DRUG ADDICTION IS INCREASING

The former UK 'drugs Tsar', appointed by the Government to solve the drugs problem said in a radio interview that the priority was to clamp down on drugs entering the country. When I pointed out that, since they can't even stop hard drugs entering our prisons, they stand no chance of preventing them entering the country, he had no coherent reply. President Bush Sr spent US $7 billion in an attempt to eliminate the supply. It had about as much effect as a spit in the ocean. Can we learn nothing from history? The prohibition experiment in 1920s USA provided us with certain valuable lessons. One was that laws should reflect the opinion of society and not the other way around. Unless they do, they will be broken. The most important lesson is if there's a demand for a product, there will always be a supply, illegal or not.

7   Banning smoking in public places

In Scotland, the ban on smoking in public places was introduced in March 2006 and is having interesting results. According to *The Sunday Times*, sales of cigarettes have gone up by 5 per cent and similar effects have been seen where other bans have been introduced, such as Spain and Ireland.[26]

Making alcohol illegal didn't solve the problem either. On the contrary, it merely created a far greater one: organized crime. In fact, the drug rings of today probably owe much of their success to the experience and training provided by the bootleggers. Even with heroin addiction, the authorities appear to attach more importance to the crime of dealing in the drug than to the misery suffered by addicts.

Because prohibition didn't cure the alcohol

problem, some so-called experts take the simplistic view that the obvious remedy is to legalize all drugs. They overlook the fact that ending prohibition didn't solve the problem either. The two drugs that cause more death, misery and destruction than all other drugs combined are both legal.

These policies have not solved the problem. You cannot remove stress or depression from the whole life of a single person, let alone the entire population. While people believe that drugs will solve or alleviate their problems, they will take them, whether they are illegal, advertised, harmful or otherwise. There remains only one solution, the one I have been advocating and proving to be successful for the last 23 years.

It needs a massive counter-brainwashing exercise to educate society generally, not about the awful side-effects of drug addiction, but about two aspects of drugs that are not generally known:

1 Drugs not only fail to achieve the object for which they are taken, but succeed in achieving the complete opposite.

2 We don't need the drugs in the first place. We are already perfectly equipped both to cope with life and enjoy it to the full.

Any businessman will tell you the one thing that will stop him manufacturing a product is if the demand ceases. If that happens, he can advertise it until the cows come home but won't even be able to give it away.

Unfortunately society spent the 20th century brainwashing our youth into believing the incalculably damaging illusion that we are basically weak and incapable of either enjoying life or coping with stress without the assistance of drugs. This has:

CREATED A MASSIVE DEMAND FOR DRUGS BOTH LEGAL AND ILLEGAL

Society has then:

SUPPLIED THEM WITH THE DRUGS THEY BELIEVE THEY NEED

Zyban, and the whole class of drugs to which it belongs, is an excellent example of how pharmaceutical companies do just this. Zyban is one of the products routinely offered at NHS stop smoking clinics, but it stands out from the rest because it is not an alternative form of nicotine. Zyban is a long-acting form of the antidepressant known as Wellbutrin.

Zyban, like Seroxat, is one of the SSRI (selective serotonin reuptake inhibitors) class of antidepressants. These drugs change the configuration of the brain by altering levels of the neurotransmitter serotonin. They are prescribed for virtually anything that has some kind of anxiety at its root. It could be for painful periods, depression, to stop smoking, to become more engaged with the world, panic attacks, irritable bowels, a weak bladder, shyness – the list is almost endless.

What is interesting about these drugs is that the

active ingredient can be the same, but the effect it has on people will depend on what is said on the label. If the drug has been shown in a clinical trial to treat irritable bowels or to help someone stop smoking, and if it has got a licence for that particular thing, then that is what it will say on the label and that is how patients will respond.

In other words, the drugs work because people have been told that they work. As such, they are a triumph of branding. What makes a smoker more likely to kick their habit on Zyban, than on the identical drug posing as an antidepressant, is the fact that this is what the doctor says, what the label says, and what the data from clinical studies supports. I agree entirely with Dr Jay Pomerantz of Harvard University who has said of this practice:

'If what we are seeing is a pattern of widespread anti-depressant prescribing for subsyndromal, amorphous patient complaints, it suggests antidepressants have become the modern-day sugar pill, or placebo... [if this is the case] taxpayers are paying the pharmaceutical industry a mighty high price for fool's gold.' [26]

They are also paying a mighty high price for the scandalous prescribing of nicotine to deal with nicotine addiction. In order to reverse the situation, we need to mount two massive counter-brainwashing campaigns, informing society of the true facts. My colleagues and I have been doing that for more than two decades and in spite of the fact that 'the Big 3' have perpetuated this brainwashing, we estimate that we have been successful in converting more than ten million smokers worldwide. If **'the Big 3'** took the trouble to absorb the contents of this book, can you see how quickly nicotine addiction could be eradicated from our planet?

If you are familiar with Easyway, in all probability you will have heard that the method doesn't work for some smokers, or alternatively that it works but not permanently. In the time allotted to me during TV, radio or newspaper articles, I've never had enough opportunity to address this issue satisfactorily. Allow me to explain why

EASYWAY WILL WORK FOR ANY SMOKER

CHAPTER 26

EASYWAY WILL WORK FOR ANY SMOKER

Assuming that the instructions are both comprehensible and correct and that the equipment isn't faulty, I assume you would agree that anyone who has no major physical or mental defects can learn to set the timer for a video recorder.

Having said that, I confess that I don't know how to set the timer for a video recorder! But that's only because I've a grandson who is willing to do it for me. However, if ever I needed to, I could certainly learn to do it myself.

In the same way, Easyway can enable any smoker to quit

EASILY, IMMEDIATELY AND PERMANENTLY!

Bear in mind that for a third of a century I was myself a victim of the brainwashing that gets smokers hooked today and I was powerless to escape. Then, on 15 July 1983, I suddenly saw the nicotine trap laid bare. I didn't need proof that I would never smoke again any more than I needed proof that someone will run better without their ankles tied together or a hood over their head. It was obvious! Nor did I doubt that the method could enable any smoker to quit. But when we set up the original clinic I did have two serious doubts:

1 Could I persuade clients to consult me?

2 Could I enable them to understand the nicotine trap and follow my instructions?

It quickly became apparent that the answer to both questions was *yes*.

Have you seen the film *Twelve Angry Men*? It must be the best film ever made in ratio of quality to cost, although there was absolutely no skimping in the quality of the cast. All twelve acted superbly. The film is so absorbing it is difficult to believe that 99 per cent is shot in just one room. A teenager is being tried for murdering his father. The case seems cut and dried. He threatened to do it, a witness claimed she saw him do it, another claimed he heard him do it: he had no effective alibi and was caught with the murder weapon on him.

Almost the entire film consists of the discussions between the various jurors, followed by a series of ballots. The result of the first ballot was eleven guilty, one not sure. The doubter, played by Henry Fonda, was not able to give any logical reason for his doubts. He even agreed that all the evidence pointed to guilt. There was just something that didn't add up – one of those cases where logic conflicts with instinct. However, this prompted another juror to point out a slight anomaly in the evidence that didn't quite add up in his mind. It was an insignificant point but prompted further discussion. Low budget the film might have been, but it is also one of the most fascinating films I have ever seen. The detective work is actually done by the jury in the jury room. At each ballot the guilty votes become fewer, until the final vote is twelve not guilty.

What actually happened in that jury room? The jurors all entered convinced the defendant was guilty. One small doubt was introduced, which led to another, then another. All twelve left unanimous and convinced he was innocent.

This is very similar to what happens at our clinics. Clients arrive tense and obviously convinced we won't be able to help them. They already know smoking is a filthy disgusting *habit* that is ruining their health and costing a fortune. That's why they seek our help; but they still believe they'll be *giving up* a genuine pleasure and/or crutch. The majority leave five hours later, not hoping for the willpower to survive the loss of their pleasure and/or crutch but seeing smoking as it really is: Devastation, and an ingenious confidence trick. They are happy they have seen through the confidence trick and have no more need to fall for it.

THEY ARE ALREADY HAPPY NON-SMOKERS!

What we do, effectively, is to remove a whole lifetime of brainwashing during a few hours. With a small minority of clients, we can't even get to first base. Others need one or more additional sessions. At the other end of the scale, occasionally after an hour or so, a client will say: *'You don't need to say another word, I can see it so clearly, I know I'll never smoke again. It's so obvious, why couldn't I see it before?'*

The clients who don't get to first base could justifiably accuse me of having failed them.

What they cannot justifiably claim is that Easyway didn't work for them.

Easyway works on exactly the same principles as the video recorder; providing you follow the instructions to the letter, neither you nor any other smoker can fail. Easyway doesn't make it easy to stop smoking. The beautiful truth is that it *is* easy to quit. It is the other methods that make it difficult. Easyway is the correct map through the smoking maze – a set of simple instructions that can guide any smoker to freedom.

Most of our clients become happy non-smokers after just one five-hour session. The last warning we give them before they leave the clinic is that in a few months they'll find it difficult to believe they were ever smokers. They'll find it even more difficult to believe they could ever get hooked again. Sometimes they try one cigarette, just to prove it to themselves. It seems to do just that, since it tastes awful. A month later they are tempted again. They think: *'I had one a month ago and didn't get hooked. Where's the harm?'* In no time at all they find themselves back in the same trap that they fell into in the first place! If they are not too embarrassed they come back to the clinic. I always ask them two questions and always get virtually the same answers.

1   *'Were you unhappy being a non-smoker?'*

'No! I loved it! I was so proud of myself.'

2   *'Do you like being a smoker again?'*

'I loathe it!'

The main object of this chapter is to point out that it's the brainwashing that gets smokers hooked and leads them to seek my help. Having successfully helped them, what happens? They go straight back into the very same environment where the brainwashing is so pervasive. I've been vehemently campaigning to change that environment for the last 23 years while **'the Big 3'** continue to perpetuate it. Can you imagine the immense frustration of then being told:

'EASYWAY DIDN'T WORK FOR ME'?

Now let me tell you about

THE INSIDIOUS GIANT OCTOPUS!

CHAPTER 27

THE INSIDIOUS GIANT OCTOPUS!

It wasn't long after I'd declared war on the tobacco industry that I sensed the presence of its sinister, covert influence. Its giant tentacles seemed to be thwarting all the attempts of anti-smoking campaigners. I'm often referred to as an anti-smoking campaigner but I do not regard myself as one. My whole object is to enable every smoker to see the confidence trick and show them just how easy and nice it is to be free of it.

The sheer ingenuity of the trap never ceases to amaze me. Even the institutions and people you would think were working for the demise of nicotine addiction seem to be working in its favour. Typical examples are **'the Big 3'**. Others are smokers who insist they are in control.

Back in the late 1970s and 1980s, I thought the *Superman* anti-smoking campaign was really effective; but I wonder how many children were influenced by those conspicuous and repeated bright red Marlboro vans and the articulated lorry bearing the Marlboro logo that featured in *Superman IV*. Do you think it was just coincidence that the filmmakers gave Marlboro that publicity or do you sense the influence of one of those invisible tentacles? Have you noticed how many comparatively recent films shown on TV fade out with a scene focusing on a cigarette or cigarette packet – usually a Marlboro packet?

Some years ago, I was informed that certain tobacco companies pay actors to smoke on screen, as well as directors and producers to feature their products in films, and also pay models to smoke in public, on photo shoots – even on the catwalk. I'm told that in the film and fashion industries this practice is common knowledge.

What's the point of banning tobacco advertising, then displaying on primetime TV macho Formula One Grand Prix cars – which actually look like packets of cigarettes – and heroic drivers wearing clothes covered with cigarette brand logos? In fact, the banning of advertising has led the tobacco industry to allocate those marketing budgets to far subtler and more effective ways of perpetuating the brainwashing. It would also appear that laws intended to protect the public against the tobacco industry are effectively doing the complete opposite. How else could it be possible for there to be a higher prevalence of smoking in Hollywood movies in 2006 than at any time since the 1950s?

In my younger days, every time a man was about to be executed in a movie, his last request was not a beautiful woman or a slap-up meal. No way. It was a cancer stick. Similarly, the crowning glory of that really special meal was not the port, the stilton or the liqueur. It was the cigar! So powerful was the brainwashing, that many non-smokers felt deprived unless they puffed on such occasions. Little did the filmmakers realize that the more expensive and larger the cigar, the more frustrating it became to regular smokers, who couldn't wait to get back to their usual brand. The miracle is how people avoided getting hooked.

Other organizations that I suspect are under the influence of the invisible tentacles are ASA and The Independent Television Commission (ITC). They purport to protect the public. As far as smoking is concerned, they achieve the complete opposite.

They inform me that they are financed by a levy from the advertisers. If so, how can they possibly describe themselves as independent? They are surely breaking their own rules and standards. The only thing they appear to be independent of is any form of logic or common sense.

When we initially opened our Birmingham clinic, we tried to advertise the fact. We were informed that the adverts did not conform to their regulations. Are you aware that one of their regulations is that you cannot advertise a quit-smoking aid that claims to work without the use of the smoker's own willpower? That might well appear to be sensible to you. It did to me. It would prevent a disreputable firm making claims they could not substantiate.

I explained that, whilst I could understand the reason for their rule, I had, in fact, discovered a method that didn't require the use of willpower and, that since more than 100,000 UK citizens had their lives short-ened every year because of smoking, weren't they participating in this slaughter by not allowing the public to become acquainted with my method?

I produced literally thousands of letters from happy ex-smokers who had quit with my method, many of them specifically stating they had not required willpower. I also produced numerous newspaper articles, which referred to the absence of willpower. I explained that the method removed the need and desire to smoke and that was why it didn't require willpower. I was told: *'To do anything requires willpower!'* I then asked if they thought it required willpower to cross the road and was told: *'Yes!'* I must admit I was slightly dumbfounded by this but it then occurred to me that to stop smoking you don't have to do anything at all, so I asked: *'If you have no desire to do something, do you believe it takes willpower not to do it?'* Incredibly, the reply was: *'Yes!'*

In case you doubt the accuracy of this dialogue, I can supply written confirmation signed by the ASA. Easyway has cured numerous top barristers. Perhaps one of them would like to take this to a judicial review so this absurd and scandalous situation can be rectified. I said:

'Look, I think you have got the wrong end of the stick. I'm not selling a poison. I'm providing a cure for the number one killer poison. I use no aids or gimmicks. It cannot possibly cause smokers any harm. The worst thing that can happen is that it doesn't work, in which case we give them their money back. If you are worried about the genuineness of the money-back guarantee, I can give references and I'm even

prepared to deposit a substantial bond with you. You are
also welcome to inspect and to investigate my records.'

They were sorry but they had their rules, laid down by experts, and it was more than their jobs were worth. I pointed out that their rules were now obsolete and their so-called experts clearly knew little about helping smokers to quit. I asked if I could be allowed to discuss the matter with these so-called experts but

I WASN'T EVEN ALLOWED TO KNOW THEIR NAMES!

It was like talking to a brick wall. In fact, it was worse. You don't expect to get a sensible response from a brick wall, but these people purport to be intelligent, caring human beings and they occupy positions of responsibility. You would think that someone whose professional duty is to protect the public would jump at the opportunity to help save the lives of over 2,000 Britons every week.

At first, these people appear helpful and suggest that you reword the advert to fit in with their stupid regulations. I pointed out that if I advertised a method that would only work with the use of willpower, but which actually didn't need willpower, I would be telling lies. Surely the ASA didn't want me to deceive the public deliberately? Strangely, that didn't seem to bother them, but on principle I refused to bend to their stupid rules. The effect was that smokers weren't allowed to know about my method. Our UK clinics still face these obstacles today.

How can we reach a state where our society will allow hundreds of millions of pounds to be spent each year promoting a poison that kills millions of smokers every year worldwide and, at the same time, prevent an isolated individual from spending a pittance to promote an effective cure for the addiction to that poison?

I got nowhere by using reason, so I tried ridicule:

'This panel of anonymous experts that you rely upon seems to understand little about smoking. Would you rely on a panel of expert ping-pong players to judge whether Nick Faldo was competent to write a book on how to play golf?'

This argument had no effect so I tried another tack. Imagine a child drowning in a boating lake. You are about to dive in to rescue it but the park keeper prevents you, saying:

'Sorry, sir, you're not allowed to swim in the lake.'

'But there's a child drowning!'

'I can see that, sir, but rules are rules. It's more than my job's worth...'

'Don't be stupid! The rules weren't meant for a situation like this.'

'Believe me, sir, the rules were drawn up by experts. They know far better than you or I.'

I'm not trying to denigrate park keepers. Such a situation could never arise. The most unimaginative, regimented, obstinate park keeper in the world would be in that lake trying to rescue the child himself. Yet when 2,000 people are drowning in the lake of cigarette smoking every week, these intelligent executives, who are highly paid to protect the public, actually use all their imagination, energy and authority to prevent me from saving them.

Can they really be that stupid? Or is there a more sinister reason for their apparent lack of initiative, imagination or common sense? How unbelievably convenient it is for the tobacco and pharmaceutical companies, that the ASA has a rule declaring you cannot advertise a quit-smoking aid that doesn't require the use of willpower. Perhaps it's really the influence of one of those hidden tentacles? Reason and ridicule got me nowhere. I asked for the matter to be taken up by someone with the authority to change these absurd rules but to no effect. Their final word was always: 'I see no point in continuing this conversation.'

I've made it clear that part of my objective is to remove the brainwashing we have been subjected to from birth: namely the illusion that we obtain some benefit and/or crutch from drugs. In order to do that we must first remove:

THE BRAINWASHING THAT CREATES THE NEED FOR DRUGS

CHAPTER 28

THE BRAINWASHING THAT CREATES THE NEED FOR DRUGS

I've described the exaltation I felt when I first discovered Easyway. Having spent a third of a century slowly and imperceptibly sliding deeper and deeper into the pit of nicotine addiction, doing a job I loathed, there I was, not only suddenly free, but actually earning my living doing something I positively loved.

I've received many compliments over the years but I must emphasize that I didn't cure those smokers out of love for my fellow man. It was for the purely selfish reason that I revelled in every minute of it. I'd always believed it's a privileged person indeed who can earn their living doing what they enjoy most. At that time I couldn't see how I could possibly be happier and as each day went by I seemed to grow in strength.

As the gunge gradually left my body, I had more energy and started to exercise. I also enjoyed not feeling so stupid for using hard-earned money to poison myself. I never expected to receive additional benefits and certainly not for them to supersede the health factor.

So obsessed had I been with resisting all the

do-gooders who were trying to force me to *give up,* that the sheer slavery of being a smoker had never occurred to me. I'd spent half my life smoking, subconsciously wishing I didn't, and the other half feeling miserable and deprived when I desperately needed a cigarette, but society or my own ego wouldn't allow me to have one.

The sheer joy of being free was overwhelming.

It was wonderful not to have to go through life feeling weak-willed and despising yourself; not having to think how your family, friends and colleagues must despise you; never having to worry if you were getting low on cigarettes or whether you would be able to get your particular brand; not having to worry whether people were smokers or non-smokers, whether your smoking would cause offence or whether the next building you entered would be non-smoking. It had never dawned on me that I avoided dental visits or smiling with my mouth open because I was ashamed of my nicotine-stained teeth.

Also, like most smokers, I blocked my mind to the ever-increasing dark shadow that hovers over all smokers. Not until I quit did I realize it had been there. It felt like a permanent burden had been removed. However, the greatest gain is the one I find most difficult to explain. Whether it was just the cumulative effect of all the other gains I don't know. I had been convinced that my packet of cigarettes was my courage.

As each day went by my inner strength grew both

physically and mentally. At 48, I was a physical and mental wreck, each morning struggling to get out of bed and suffering a permanent feeling of foreboding, wondering how I would get through each day. My state of mind was so low that I was actually prepared to die rather than *give up* smoking.

The last 23 years have been the best of my life. I rarely stay in bed after seven in the morning and I wake up rested, full of excitement and looking forward to the challenges that each day brings. It's as if I never properly matured until after I escaped from the nicotine trap; as I got hooked during adolescence that is probably the case. How much harder for the youth of today, many of whom are hooked in childhood – and not only on nicotine and alcohol.

This week I learned that I've contracted lung cancer. The doctors estimate I have nine months to live. Naturally the news was a shock. Please be assured that I'm not looking for sympathy. The beautiful truth is I don't need it. I couldn't even say the word 23 years ago. Today, it holds no terrors for me whatsoever. I was in pain at first, but the doctors and nurses at Epsom General Hospital and The Royal Marsden have been wonderful and have the situation under control. The truth is I feel great!

I've had such a wonderful life with more happiness than just one person has a right to expect. I have no intention of sitting around waiting to die and intend to live each day to the full, as I have since I escaped from the nicotine trap. My mission in life is to see the beginning of the end of nicotine addiction before I die.

If you can help me achieve that ambition, I'll die a very happy man.

Do you think that creatures like tigers and elephants are weak compared to a human being? In Western society, the birth of a child is not just a hospitalization job for most mothers and babies, but requires both prenatal and postnatal care. Mother and baby need regular visits from doctors and healthcare workers and the baby needs injections against a variety of diseases. Children are taught not to go out in the rain and to keep well wrapped up. At the slightest sign of illness or fever, the child visits the doctor or vice versa. It's often not until the child is at least twelve years old that it is even capable of surviving independently of its parents or an institution.

The point I'm making is that compared to tigers and elephants, we think of ourselves as incredibly fragile. Yet, we are made of the same flesh and blood as tigers and elephants, which, ironically, are both in danger of extinction. We, on the other hand, equipped with our superior brains, have been so successful that our proliferation is the reason so many other species have become extinct.

I'm not suggesting we change our ways in relation to childbirth. What I am saying is that while I smoked I had this feeling of fragility, and that after I quit it gradually left me and was replaced by a growing feeling of confidence. Am I saying I've closed my eyes to my condition? On the contrary, I've accepted it. I'm not just strong enough to accept it, but also to handle it.

Many clients have written to me saying something like: *'You not only saved my life, but changed my life for the better in so many ways!'*

Although we do not cover this point at our clinics, let me describe:

THE MIND-OPENING PROCESS THAT FOLLOWED MY ESCAPE

CHAPTER 29

THE MIND-OPENING PROCESS THAT FOLLOWED MY ESCAPE

I was born into a working-class family in south-west London. We were classified Church of England, although, like the majority of our neighbours, my parents only attended church for weddings, funerals and christenings. I'm a religious person, but do not worship nor am I attached to any specific faith. In fact, my religious convictions do not require faith; on the contrary, they are firmly based on fact. I believe in the Ten Commandments, not because I'm religious but because they are a basic set of rules that enable all people of whatever race, creed or colour to live in peace and harmony together. I also learned at an early age to believe in Jiminy Cricket's slogan: *Let your conscience be your guide*.

The subject I'm about to discuss is religious. I, therefore, make it clear that I have no prejudice against any established or private religious beliefs. In no way am I trying to force my beliefs on you. In fact, I believe that what I am about to say will not be in conflict with anyone who wishes to live in peace and happiness with their neighbours, whether they are a member of an established religion, an atheist or an agnostic.

Like my fellow street urchins, I was regularly dispatched to Sunday School every Sunday afternoon – until I was expelled. This was not so much to ensure I received religious instruction, but to allow my father to sleep off in peace the effects of the Sunday roast and the several pints of beer that had preceded it.

I cannot remember at what stage I ceased to believe in the tooth fairy, Father Christmas and the like, but to lose faith in God just seemed like a natural progression. Like my parents, I continued to attend church only for weddings, funerals and christenings, purely because it was the culture of my family and friends. To all intents and purposes I had closed my mind to all matters religious. Not only did I not believe in God but I had no need to. I suppose my god was the combined ingenuity of mankind and the belief in his ability to solve all problems.

I spoke earlier of an inner strength that grew inside me after I stopped smoking. I first became aware of it during a mental block. There was this magnificent oak tree immediately outside my window and whenever I had a mental block I would stare at it hoping for inspiration. I've described it as magnificent, but I had never seen it that way. In fact, I didn't even know it was an oak tree. It was just a tree like any other tree, very nice, but no big deal.

On that day I saw it, as if for the first time, as a miracle of nature. Just consider it for a moment. A tiny acorn falls to the ground, gets swallowed by a pig and is fortunate enough to be deposited where it can germinate and grow into a mighty oak that can live for a thousand years.

Each year it produces a magnificent display of leaves to raise our spirits in spring. Even in autumn when they fall, the leaves produce an aura of reds and golds and help fertilize the soil for future generations. Each year, the tree produces thousands of acorns and it takes just one acorn in any one year to germinate and grow to ensure the future of the species in perpetuity. The remaining acorns serve as food for many species and the oak itself serves as a home and nourishment for many more.

Yet, that tree is completely independent of mankind; nobody waters it or nourishes it. Nobody? Has modern man become so obsessed with his own technological achievements that he believes that anything that happens independently of him is mere chance? So who did water and nurture it? I don't know and have no intention of speculating.

As I said, I'm not dealing in faith but in fact. I don't pretend to understand the miracles of Mother Nature and I cannot deny I closed my eyes to them for half a century. But now that I've opened my eyes and my mind, I cannot deny that they exist

AND NOR CAN YOU!

Of course, evolution explains how the oak tree evolved from more simple plants. Evolution is a fact and works in the same way as the modern Rolls-Royce evolved from the wheel, but while man may have learned to split cells and create destruction on a massive scale, he cannot create a single living cell, let alone something as incredibly sophisticated as an acorn. Just think of it:

'Attention class, today's task is to invent the acorn, it's really quite simple. You can use whatever materials you think necessary, but they mustn't weigh more than half an ounce. Then you merely place your acorn in soil and you mustn't interfere with it again and the object is that after ten years your acorn must be as tall as a house.'

Also remember that the acorn itself is just a tiny part of an ecosystem that has enabled a countless variety of species to survive for over three billion years. Mankind has been on earth less than one million years and is the only species that threatens the existence of the entire planet. Perhaps you are wondering what all this has to do with achieving my objective. If so, let me remind you that people fall into the drugs trap as the direct result of two illusions. The first is the belief that whatever intelligence created us, it left us flawed to the extent that we cannot enjoy life to the full or effectively handle stress without the aid of drugs. I'm not referring here to drugs prescribed by doctors to treat a specific medical condition. However, the tendency of the medical profession to prescribe drugs that treat symptoms – rather than remove the root cause of conditions – has undoubtedly exacerbated the problem of the drugs to which I am referring, such as nicotine, alcohol and heroin, which people take in the mistaken belief that they provide some genuine pleasure or crutch.

The following is the second illusion. It's all very well to explain to a smoker that the nicotine trap is an ingenious confidence trick, and smoking provides no genuine pleasure or crutch whatsoever. But for years, the smoker has regarded the cigarette as his friend. Many start so young nowadays they cannot remember life without it. It leaves a void, rather like discovering the person they thought to be their best friend is actually their worst enemy. They still feel they've lost their best friend!

It is essential to remove both illusions, not just to explain why all addictive drugs are merely confidence tricks providing no genuine pleasure or crutch, but also to show that the intelligence that created us has already equipped us with all the drugs we need, both to enjoy life to the full and to cope with stress. Please bear with me. What I've written above was merely the start of the mind-opening process. Let's take a look at

THE INCREDIBLE MACHINE

CHAPTER 30

THE INCREDIBLE MACHINE

I began to compare my body to that oak tree. When I was a child, I would bleed profusely from cuts. This frightened me. No one explained to me that bleeding was, in fact, a natural and essential healing process and that the blood would clot when its healing purpose was completed. I suspected I was a haemophiliac and feared I might bleed to death. Later in life, as a smoker, I would sustain quite deep cuts yet hardly bleed at all. A brownish-red gunge would ooze out.

The colour worried me. I knew blood was meant to be bright red and I assumed I had some sort of blood disease. However, I was pleased about the consistency, which meant that I no longer bled profusely. Not until after I had stopped smoking did I learn that smoking coagulates the blood and that the brownish colour was due to lack of oxygen. I was ignorant of the effect at the time but, in hindsight, it was this effect of smoking on my health that most fills me with horror. When I think of my poor heart trying to pump that gunge around restricted blood vessels, day after day, without missing a single beat, I find it a miracle I didn't suffer a stroke or a major heart attack. It made me realize, not how fragile our bodies are, but how strong and ingenious that incredible machine is!

For a third of a century, I had been continually inhaling one of the most powerful poisons known to mankind. At the same time, I had treated my stomach like a waste disposal unit, shoving food into my mouth oblivious as to its health content, and using regular supplies of indigestion and constipation tablets to dispose of the waste. How incredibly strong my body must have been to survive, let alone suffer no major illness.

Many smokers who consulted other types of therapists before me complain that they are questioned about their early childhood. They find this rather annoying because they cannot see the significance of the questions. They are absolutely correct. In order to understand the nicotine trap fully, you need to go back further – over three billion years – when life on earth first developed. The human body is the result of three billion years of trial and error and is by far the most sophisticated and powerful survival machine on the planet.

It felt as if I had discovered this incredibly powerful machine:

THE HUMAN BODY

And in particular:

THE HUMAN BRAIN

I have total belief that this machine is better equipped to handle any situation without drugs.

It wasn't the machine itself I had discovered; that had been there all my life. But like most of the really important things in life – food, freedom, security, good health, employment, love and friendship – when we have them, we tend either to take them for granted or to complain about their quality. It's only when we are deprived that we truly appreciate them. When I was a teenager, I was aware of the physical power and strength of that body, but at the age of 48 it had become physically and mentally rundown. I was aware my heavy smoking wasn't helping the physical side, but society had brainwashed me to believe that old age was a terminal disease in any case.

Let's just pause a moment to consider the incredible sophistication of our bodies. Can you do the ironing, make the bed, answer the phone, do the shopping and clean the car? Of course you can. But could you perform all those tasks at the same time? Now, consider the thousands of tasks our bodies perform automatically, all at the same time, even as we sleep. Our heart has to keep pumping, never missing a single beat. Blood must carry energy and nutrients to every part of our body. Our internal thermostat has to maintain both our internal and external temperatures to the correct levels. Every one of our organs – our liver, lungs and kidneys – has to function. Our stomach must digest our food; our intestines must distinguish between food and waste, extract the former and arrange disposal of the latter – preferably not while we sleep.

Any good doctor will tell you that your greatest ally in fighting infection and disease is not him nor any drugs he can prescribe, but your immune system, which links with your endocrine and nervous systems to supply chemicals like adrenalin and dopamine to the correct part of your body and in the quantities required.

Our knowledge of the human body has expanded a thousandfold in the last hundred years. We can transplant organs and achieve mind-boggling results with genetic engineering. However, the greatest experts on these subjects admit that this increased insight into the functioning of the human body makes them realize how little we understand about its workings. All too often, it has been shown that, in the long run, the interventions we undertake with our limited knowledge cause many more problems than they solve. If your highly sophisticated computer developed a fault, would you let a gorilla try to fix it?

One scientist described unfolding knowledge about the workings of the human body as clearing a space approximately 12 feet in circumference in the centre of a huge forest. Clear another yard all round and you now have a circumference of over 30 feet. Clear just one more yard and you are now confronted by a circumference of 50 feet.

By far, the most powerful survival machine on the planet is the human body. It is a million times more sophisticated than the most powerful spacecraft made by mankind. If the oil in my car shows the slightest discoloration, I have it changed. But if I had treated my car as I abused my body for the first 48 years of my life, I doubt it would have lasted much more than a year.

The human body is the culmination of more than three billion years of trial and error all designed to achieve one object and one object alone:

SURVIVAL

Three billion years is an awful lot of research and when so-called intelligent man contradicts the laws of Mother Nature, without knowing the exact consequences of his actions

HE IS CERTAINLY NOT BEING INTELLIGENT

Our every instinct and guiding force is to ensure we survive. I used to think fear was a form of weakness or cowardice. But without a fear of fire, of heights, of drowning or of being attacked, we would not survive.

At our clinics smokers often say: *'I suffer with my nerves,'* as if feeling nervous were a disease. The door slams and you jump two feet in the air. That isn't bad nerves; that's good nerves. Watch starlings feeding. They appear oblivious to what's happening around them, but the slightest sound will cause them to fly off as one. That sound signifies 'DANGER' and it's the starling that doesn't react instantly that risks falling prey to a predator.

We think of tiredness and pain as evils. On the contrary, they are warning lights. Tiredness is your body telling you that you need to rest. Pain is telling you that part of your body is being attacked and remedial action is necessary. There are people born without the ability to feel pain or sense danger and they find it very difficult to survive. If they rest their arm on a hot stove, it's not until they smell their flesh burning that they become aware of the problem.

So much of established modern medicine is obsessed with treating the symptoms of diseases rather than the causes. Take my own case – typical Sod's law. I spent half my life damaging my throat because I smoked and, having successfully quit, the rest of my life damaging it because I spent so much time talking about smoking. I used to get regular sore throats because I talked too much. My wife, Joyce, got me anaesthetic sprays or tablets. The pain went and I thought: *'What marvellous stuff'*. It isn't. The sore throat wasn't the problem; it was my body telling me: *'Give your voice a rest! If you don't you are going to cause bigger problems.'*

By anaesthetizing the pain, all I really achieved was the equivalent of removing the oil warning light on the car dashboard instead of topping up the oil. I then did the one thing that I shouldn't have done, I went on talking. In addition, by removing the symptoms, I have also removed the signals to my brain, which would have triggered my immune system. I have effectively disarmed the most powerful and efficient healing force on the planet:

THE IMMUNE SYSTEM

We think of hunger and thirst as evils. On the contrary, they are alarm bells. Your body is warning you that unless you eat and drink, you will not survive. Each of our senses is designed to ensure we survive. We're equipped with eyes to see danger; ears to hear danger; a nose to smell it; touch to feel hot or sharp surfaces; and taste to know the difference between food and poison.

Many doctors have now discovered that drugs such as antidepressants cause more problems than they solve. These substances have a similar effect to alcohol – they take the patient's mind off their problems, but they don't cure them. When the effect has worn off, another dose is required. Because the drugs themselves are poisons, they have physical and mental side-effects and the body builds a tolerance to them, so that its blocking effect is reduced. The addict now has the original stress, plus the additional physical and mental stress caused by being dependent on a drug that is supposed to be relieving them.

Eventually the body builds up such a tolerance that the drug ceases to give even an illusion of relieving stress. All too often, the remedy is now either to administer larger and more frequent doses of the same drug, or to upgrade the patient to an even more powerful one. The whole process is an ever-accelerating plunge down a bottomless pit.

Some doctors try to justify the use of such drugs by maintaining that they prevent the patient from having a nervous breakdown. Again, they try to remove the symptoms. A nervous breakdown isn't a disease; on the contrary, it's a partial cure and another warning light. It is nature's way of saying: *'I can't cope with any more stress, responsibility or problems. I've had it up to here. I need a rest. I need a break!'*

The problem is that many people often take on too much responsibility. Everything is fine whilst they are in control and can handle it. In fact, they frequently thrive on it. However, everyone has phases in life when a series of problems coincide. Observe politicians when they are campaigning to become president or prime minister. They are strong, rational, decisive and positive. They have simple solutions to all our problems. But when they achieve their ambition, you can hardly recognize them as the same person. Now they have the *actual* responsibility of office, they become negative and hesitant.

No matter how weak or strong we are, we all have bad patches in our lives. The natural tendency at such times is to seek solace in our traditional crutches: *alcohol, tobacco or other drugs.* I say *natural* tendency but there's absolutely nothing *natural* about it! We've been brainwashed from birth. With many fallen idols, like Alex 'Hurricane' Higgins and George Best, it is blatantly obvious that chemical dependence has not helped their problems, but is in itself the cause of their downfall. So it was with me, but I couldn't see it either.

The only answer to stress is to remove the cause; it's pointless trying to pretend it doesn't exist. Whether the stress is real or mainly illusory, drugs will make the reality and the illusion worse. Another problem is that we are also brainwashed into believing we lead stressful lives. The truth is that the human species has successfully removed most of the causes of genuine stress. We no longer have the fear of being attacked by wild animals every time we leave our homes and the vast majority of us don't have to worry about where our next meal will come from or whether we'll have a roof over our heads.

How would you like to be a rabbit? Every time you pop your head out of the burrow, you not only have the problem of searching for food, but you have to avoid becoming the next meal of another creature. Even back in your burrow you cannot relax or feel secure, as you are at risk from floods, ferrets and myriad other hazards. The stress of serving in the Vietnam War, understandably, caused many servicemen to turn to drugs. But they served for a comparatively short period. A rabbit lives through a 'Vietnam' its whole life, yet still manages to procreate at a prolific rate and feed its family. The average rabbit even looks happier than the average human!

The reason rabbits can take all these traumas in their stride is because they have adrenalin and other drugs occurring naturally. The creator has also equipped them with sight, smell, hearing, touch and instinct, in fact, with everything they need to survive. Rabbits are wonderful survival machines.

BUT THE VERY BEST ARE HUMAN BEINGS

Fortunately the creator did not neglect us. We have reached a stage of evolution where we can even partly control the elements themselves. Properly organized, we could eliminate the effects of drought, flood or earthquake. We have just one substantial enemy to conquer:

OUR OWN STUPIDITY

We lay down standards that we try to achieve. A select few seem to achieve them all. The Richard Burtons, the Elizabeth Taylors of this world appear to have everything going for them. They are physically and mentally strong. What destroys them? Their jobs? Old age? The normal stresses of life? None of these. What destroys them are the illusory crutches that they turn to: nicotine, alcohol and similar poisons.

At our clinics we ask smokers: *'Do you have a smoker's cough?'* Often the reply is: *'I would stop smoking if I did.'* A cough isn't a disease. On the contrary, it is another of nature's survival techniques, to eject harmful deposits from the lungs. Just as vomiting is another survival technique, to eject poisons from our stomachs.

Imagine flying over the Alps in blanket fog. You'd be entirely dependent upon your instruments: altimeter, radar, speedometer, fuel gauge, compass and so on. Even if they were all functioning properly, it would still be a very scary business indeed, particularly if you had a fear of flying as I once did.

Your body, equipped with your brain, is the vehicle you are dependent on for a long, happy and healthy life. For a moment, try to imagine life without your senses: you cannot see, hear, smell, taste or even touch. Effectively, you wouldn't exist.

You are now back in the fog over the Alps and notice that your altitude has dropped to 8,000 feet. Knowing that the taller peaks are in excess of 16,000 feet, you wouldn't feel safe until your altitude was a greater height than the tallest peak, plus a margin for error. What would you think of some idiot who said:

'Why don't you just adjust the calibration on your altimeter to read 18,000 feet?'

That would be even more stupid than removing the oil warning light rather than topping up the oil, or replacing a fuse with a nail because it kept blowing.

Obviously, there is no point in taking a drug unless it's going to have some effect, which means that you are automatically altering the calibration of one or more of your senses, which are the instruments on which your well-being depends. A classic example is drinking and driving.

The biggest idiot on earth wouldn't dream of altering the correct working of his instruments, whether he was flying over the Alps in blanket fog or at any other time. Yet that is effectively what we do when we take drugs.

The increased feeling of security, courage, confidence and happiness I've experienced over the last 23 years has not just come from the multiple benefits of having escaped from the nicotine trap. It has also come from the certain knowledge that whatever intelligence or process created the human body has also provided us with all we need, both to enjoy life to the full and to cope with stress.

Have you heard the expression:

THE MAJORITY IS ALWAYS WRONG?

CHAPTER 31

THE MAJORITY IS ALWAYS WRONG

I first heard the expression forty years ago in the company of friends. It started a heated discussion and I argued vehemently that the statement was obviously nonsense. Surely, the more brains that agree with a particular point of view, the greater the chance of that view being correct?

It wasn't until the following day – the brain no longer affected by alcohol – that the other man's statement began to make sense. The point he was trying to make is this: if a thousand people all agree a particular point and just one person argues the opposite, that one person will probably be right. Why? Because unless that person is a complete fool, he would not contradict the unanimous view of a thousand others without being absolutely certain he was right. In any case, fools tend not to contradict the unanimous view of the vast majority but simply to go along with them. Little did I know that, years later, I would be a lone individual contradicting the entire established medical profession. Perhaps you still find it difficult to accept my claim. However, before you reject it, please consider the following facts.

When I started my bid to cure the world of smoking, I was alone. There are now millions who agree with me. True, that is still a small minority of the world's population, but the majority has not yet had the opportunity to understand, and this is the cause of my frustration and the reason for writing this book. I've already proved that all smokers want to quit, and Easyway can enable each and every one of them to do so. If details of Easyway had been circulated around the world in 1983, I believe smoking would have been reduced to the same low level as snuff-taking occupies today.

I know that the policies of 'the Big 3' seem logical, and that's part of the ingenuity of the nicotine trap; until you understand it, everything seems to be the opposite of what it actually is. 'The Big 3' focus on the reasons we shouldn't smoke but people are well aware of these and they don't smoke for the reasons that they shouldn't smoke. We need to remove the illusions that make them continue to smoke despite the obvious disadvantages. While smokers, ex-smokers and even some lifelong non-smokers believe that smoking provides a genuine pleasure or crutch and is merely a habit, nicotine addiction will continue to thrive – particularly when the drug is supplied freely on the NHS via so-called nicotine replacement therapy

The fact that many smokers welcome smoking bans merely confuses the issue. I deliberately took a job in a non-smoking office in the belief it would force me to quit. Like many of my willpower attempts, it was fine to start with. But then I had one of those days, bought some cigarettes and had a crafty smoke in the toilet. I soon reached the stage where I might just as well have moved my desk into the toilet!

Look at the facts. Stand outside any school at the end of the school day and you'll see children blatantly puffing away as if a cigarette is the greatest thing on earth. I repeat:

THE WORLD HEALTH ORGANIZATION HAS PREDICTED THAT BY 2020 ANNUAL DEATHS FROM SMOKING WILL HAVE DOUBLED FROM FIVE MILLION TO TEN MILLION WORLDWIDE

Many parents cannot believe what they consider to be the stupidity of their children who, having been warned of the risks, still fall into the trap. But the trap is ingenious, the health scares pose no immediate threat and no youngster ever believes they'll get hooked.

Perhaps you believe that even if the trap is explained to them, many will still get hooked. That isn't our experience at the clinics and that applies when all the other so-called experts are still perpetuating the illusion.

A minority of clients have difficulty understanding Easyway in one session. There will often be a conversation similar to the following:

Client: *I understood everything you said but it didn't seem to work for me.*

Therapist: Would you place your hands in boiling water

just to get the relief of removing them?

Client: *Of course not!*

Therapist: Then you haven't understood everything I've said.

If it were possible to explain to a fish that hidden inside that wriggling, juicy worm is a vicious steel barb, do you think it would swallow the bait?

If you explain to the insect exactly how the pitcher plant works, do you think it would fall for the trap?

If you could explain to a mouse that if it tried to nibble that piece of cheese, a great iron bar would swing down and break its back, do you think it would nibble it?

Now please re-read my definition of Devastation:

DEVASTATION is an extract from a plant indigenous to South America, of the same family as deadly nightshade (Solanaceae). It is the most addictive drug known to mankind. Over 60 per cent of adults become hooked. It is a powerful poison and is used commercially as an insecticide. It gradually breaks down the immune system, causes breathlessness and lethargy and, according to latest medical statistics, kills one in two of those who are unfortunate enough to become addicted. It tastes foul and systematically destroys the nervous system, causing a feeling of insecurity and a lack of

confidence. It currently costs the average UK addict around £100,000 over a lifetime.

What does it do for them?

ABSOLUTELY NOTHING!

Our children aren't the fools we take them for. If, instead of brainwashing them to believe nicotine relaxes them, helps them to concentrate and relieves stress and boredom, we were to explain how it does the complete reverse and that just one cigarette or piece of nicotine gum can hook you.

DO YOU THINK THEY'D STILL FALL FOR IT?

PLEASE AT LEAST HELP ME GIVE THEM THE OPPORTUNITY TO FIND OUT

So far I've concentrated on nicotine addiction. Let's now take a closer look at:

HEROIN ADDICTION

CHAPTER 32

HEROIN ADDICTION

The first time I heard of anything like heroin addiction was my geography master's description of Chinamen lying around all day smoking special pipes in gloomy opium houses, in order to have wonderful psychedelic dreams. The picture he painted was absolute anathema to me and I just couldn't understand anyone reaching that stage of addiction.

Consequently, I'd formed the impression that heroin addicts went through the horror of obtaining heroin and injecting themselves just to experience marvellous dreams. But let me ask you, when you go to bed at night, do you lie there praying that you'll have marvellous dreams or are you, like me, just grateful not to have nightmares and happy to settle for a dreamless night?

Picture a heroin addict who is overdue for his next dose and the agitation he's going through. Now think of the relief when he finally gets his fix and can end that awful craving. Do you really believe he injects himself to have marvellous dreams or isn't it in order to end that awful craving? Non-heroin addicts don't have that awful craving any more than non-smokers crave cigarettes. Each dose, far from relieving the agony, is a one-way journey to a bottomless pit.

When I discovered Easyway, I related it only to nicotine. The only other drug I'd had personal experience of was alcohol, and at that time I didn't regard alcohol as addictive.

It was during a group session that the penny first dropped. One of the participants announced that he was a recovering alcoholic. Immediately, another confessed he was one too, shortly followed by another who admitted to being an ex-heroin addict. It seemed the entire group had been hooked on something and some of them had been hooked on everything going.

At the time, I thought it was a very exceptional group, but later I learned it wasn't so exceptional after all. I was intrigued. I'd always believed that the really difficult one to kick was heroin. Yet here were all these people – who had managed to kick not just heroin but also alcohol, cocaine and other drugs – unable to quit smoking without my help; and all insisting that nicotine was the really difficult one.

I asked them to describe the terrible withdrawal pangs from heroin. The answer was a revelation, as it was very similar to how smokers described quitting on willpower. It dawned on me that, although the trap varies slightly with each drug, all work the same confidence trick and once you can see through that trick, you no longer fall for it.

Traditionally, nicotine and alcohol are the drugs youngsters first dabble in. Nicotine is simplicity itself.

When nicotine leaves your body, you feel insecure; when you light up, that feeling seems to be relieved. Alcohol has a two-pronged effect. The first is that it deadens all your senses and you begin to lose your fears and inhibitions, which leaves you oblivious to danger. The second prong is that, far from quenching your thirst as many people believe, alcohol actually dehydrates you. This is why a glass of water will normally satisfy your thirst, but some drinkers will drink eight pints of beer and still wake up in the middle of the night with a throat like a dried-up river bed.

Although we might dabble with alcohol before nicotine, because of the different nature of the two drugs, addiction to alcohol usually doesn't set in until the drinker is using it regularly to block problems from his or her mind. With smoking, addiction sets in very quickly. It's not long after you notice a youngster experimenting with cigarettes that he is buying his own and smoking regularly.

It's regarded as quite normal for a smoker to light up first thing in the morning, whereas a drinker who did the same would be regarded as an alcoholic. It is nicotine that plants this seed in our bodies and minds, suggesting we are incomplete and need something to fill the void. What people fail to realize is that:

NICOTINE CREATES THAT VOID

Nicotine therefore creates the conditions that often lead to other drugs. Once you have belief in the ability of your mind and body both to enjoy life to the full and cope with stress effectively, all drugs cease to be necessary or desirable.

I should make it clear that when I refer to *all drugs*, I refer only to so-called *recreational* drugs like nicotine, alcohol, heroin and cocaine, and not to drugs prescribed by your doctor for medicinal purposes – although, in fact, the same does apply to many of these as well.

We are now in a position to draw some far-reaching conclusions.

CHAPTER 33

PLEASE HELP ME END THIS SCANDAL

In the relatively short period that mankind has been on the planet and, as our incredible technology advances, we are rushing headlong in several directions that risk destroying the planet we depend upon.

We've used our ingenuity to create bombs so powerful we daren't use them. We are polluting our land, lakes, rivers and seas, even the air we breathe. We are using up our natural resources at a frightening rate. We are over-cultivating our land; depleting our reserves of fish; creating holes in the ozone layer; chopping down rainforests at a frightening rate; and creating global warming. We still haven't learned to live in peace or anything approaching harmony.

Some people have such faith in the ingenuity of mankind they believe we'll find solutions to these problems, rather like the man who has just fallen from a hundred storey skyscraper. As he hurtles past the tenth floor he says:

'So far so good!'

I don't pretend to know the solution but I too believe in the ingenuity of mankind and in our ability to use our intelligence to improve our lot. There is one great problem we *can* do something about now, by releasing our children and grandchildren from the belief that they are incomplete and cannot enjoy life to the full or cope with life effectively, without the use of drugs.

We can do that by informing them of the true facts about smoking. Not that it's a filthy, disgusting *habit* that will ruin their health and cost them a fortune. We've been doing that for over half a century and it hasn't worked. We should explain that it's a confidence trick and that's why they'll enjoy life so much more, and be better able to cope with stress, while they are free from the slavery; and how every smoker can quit easily, immediately and permanently!

This is the last book I will write. My protégé and successor, the Worldwide Head of Easyway, Robin Hayley, has already started the first project that is likely to be released after my death. This will deliver guidance and education to children and parents on how to avoid the smoking trap.

We have just one problem: three powerful institutions who continue to perpetuate myths and illusions about smoking, all of whom are influenced by powerful pharmaceutical companies, which have a huge financial interest in perpetuating nicotine addiction.

It takes a brave man to admit he is wrong, but whether you are a politician, a doctor, a scientist or a member of the media, I'm asking you to examine your conscience and at least examine my claims. Once a few really influential people demonstrate the courage and integrity it takes, word will spread like wildfire!

When my wife, Joyce, and I started the first clinic in Raynes Park, London, I was in the practice of following up each client after a few days to check on progress. On one occasion, the client confirmed he was doing fine and had no problems. I'd hardly put the phone down when I got a call from his wife: *'Would you mind having a chat with my husband? He keeps sneaking out to the garage and I'm sure he's having crafty puffs.'*

I said he had just assured me he was doing fine. I was in a quandary. I could hardly ring him and question his word. But I was saved by the bell. He was back on the phone and admitted he was having problems. Fortunately, he came back for a second appointment and was successful. However, the incident proved that you cannot trust the word of a drug addict and I've already made the point that it is impossible to prove that someone doesn't smoke.

We are well aware that there are some clients who fail and don't bother to claim their money back. During the eight years that ended 31 December 2005, our audited accounts confirm that fewer than 7 per cent of our clients found it necessary to claim under our guarantee. I am not aware of any serious rival who is prepared to offer a money back guarantee on a cure for smoking, let alone one which satisfies more than 93 per cent of clients. You might think there is always small print on guarantees, which make it difficult to claim. This might well apply to insurance companies, but I did not achieve my reputation by trying to cheat clients. There are no forms to complete and we take the client's word.

My books have sold more than ten million copies and I have a worldwide network of clinics in which, during 2005 alone, we treated 45,000 smokers.

NICE has recently been under attack for refusing to advocate certain apparently effective drugs on the grounds that they are not cost-effective. It would appear that in the case of Western society's number one killer disease, they have completely reversed this role. They are actually advocating NRT on the basis of statistics which are meaningless, since the substance perpetuates the addiction smokers are trying to break free from. And yet, a method that has been shown to break nicotine addiction is not even evaluated, let alone reimbursed, on the NHS.

A NATIONAL SCANDAL ON A GIGANTIC SCALE!

Easyway has not had the benefit of charitable donations, government funding or the vast wealth of the pharmaceutical companies to fund marketing campaigns. The success and fame of its method has been achieved through personal recommendations. I am now recognized as the world's leading expert on helping smokers to quit for one reason alone:

MY METHOD WORKS

The fact that fewer than 10 per cent of our clients find it necessary to claim under our guarantee is a remarkable and easily verifiable statistic and one I never expected to achieve whilst **'the Big 3'** and society generally continue to perpetuate the illusions and myths listed in the appendix. I'm convinced that once those illusions are shattered, the incidence of smoking in society will rapidly fall to the level that snuff-taking occupies today.

However, we possess another testament, which in my opinion is the greatest endorsement of all. I have asked hundreds of people: *'Have you ever written to an author?'* To date, not one person has answered *'Yes'*. I've received literally thousands of letters of thanks from satisfied clients over the years and the pile grows every year. Those letters convey more than any bare statistics exactly why, compared to Easyway, other methods are like trying to run with your ankles tied together. You can check out thousands of such messages from happy non-smokers who have used the method on http://www.allen-carr.com, all of them stating just how EASY it was.

Even if you are not a member of **'the Big 3'**, I'm begging you for your help to end this SCANDAL. No doubt you already have friends or relatives who are in the trap, or children or grandchildren who may be vulnerable. Don't just talk about it. Lobby your MP, your doctor, your newspaper, radio station or TV network and internet sites and insist on knowing why they are still advocating methods that don't work or don't prevent youngsters getting hooked; and ignoring one that does. Also pass this book on to your friends and persuade them to join the cause.

In many programmes and articles, emphasis is placed on the fortune I have made out of helping smokers to quit. Would these people make the same point about eminent heart surgeons, top medical specialists and the like? These same programmes and articles omit to mention the billions of pounds our Government continues to extract from the hapless smoker; the hundreds of millions extracted from the taxpayer to fund the failing NHS stop smoking programmes; the billions the pharmaceutical companies are making by selling nicotine; or the massive advertising revenues the media earns from them. How ironic that the media seem more concerned with how much I've earned, or how many celebrities have sought my help, than the incredible potential of my discovery. I'm not ashamed that my enterprise is profitable; it has to be in order to survive, but I'm prepared to spend every penny I own if you can help me see the end of this SCANDAL before I die.

Thank you,
Allen Carr

Allen Carr passed away in November 2006. However, his legacy remains in the form of his worldwide organization which continues his work. If you wish to support this cause, please send your name and address to:

Allen Carr's Easyway
The Nicotine Conspiracy
Park House
14 Pepys Rd
London SW20 8NH

or to: thenicotineconspiracy@allencarr.com

FINAL TRIBUTE

To Joyce:
Behind every great man you'll find a great woman.
Behind this rather mediocre specimen you'll find a
truly extraordinary woman!

REFERENCES

1 Moshammer, H., Neuberger, M., 'Long-term success of short smoking-cessation seminars supported by occupational health care', *Addictive Behaviors*, 2006

2 Hutter, H.P., Moshammer, H., Neuberger, M., 'Smoking cessation at the workplace: one year success of short seminars', *Internal Archives of Occupational Environmental Health*, 2005

3 Polito, John R., 'The NRT cessation charade continues', *British Medical Journal*, 23 February 2004

4 *Securing good health for the whole population* [The Wanless Report], HM Treasury, 25 February 2004

5 Etter, Jean-François, Stapleton, John A., 'Nicotine replacement therapy for long-term smoking cessation: a meta-analysis', *Tobacco Control*, 2006; 15; 280–5

6 Law, Jacky, *Big Pharma*, Constable & Robinson, London, 2006, p.28

7 *The influence of the pharmaceutical industry* (Report of the House of Commons Health Committee) 5 April 2005, p.3

8 *The influence of the pharmaceutical industry* (Report of the House of Commons Health Committee) 5 April 2005, p.3

9 *The influence of the pharmaceutical industry* (Report of the House of Commons Health Committee) 5 April 2005, para. 158

10 Law, Jacky, *Big Pharma*, Constable & Robinson, London, 2006, p.23

11 Heath, Iona, 'A wolf in sheep's clothing: a critical look at the ethics of drug taking', *British Medical Journal*, 2003, 327: 856–8

12 *The influence of the pharmaceutical industry* (Report of the House of Commons Health Committee) 5 April 2005, paras 339–40

13 Angell, Dr Marcia, *The Truth About the Drug Companies*, Random House, New York, 2004, p.48

14 Waxman, Henry A., 'The lessons of Vioxx', *New England Journal of Medicine*, 23 June 2005, p.2576

15 Horton, Richard, *MMR: Science & Fiction: Exploring the Vaccine Crisis*, Granta, London, 2004, p.81

16 Horton, Richard, *MMR: Science & Fiction: Exploring the Vaccine Crisis*, Granta, London, 2004, p.82

17 Jacky Law, *Big Pharma*, Constable & Robinson, London, 2006, p.47

18 Jacky Law, *Big Pharma*, Constable & Robinson, London, 2006, p.35

19 *The influence of the pharmaceutical industry* (Report of the House of Commons Health Committee) 5 April 2005, para. 299

20 Martinez, Barbara, 'New York Attorney General accuses Glaxo of fraud', *Wall Street Journal*, European ed., 3 June 2004

21 Parrott, Steve, Godfrey, Christine, 'Economics of smoking cessation', *British Medical Journal*, 17 April 2004

22 *The influence of the pharmaceutical industry* (Report of the House of Commons Health Committee)

5 April 2005, para. 142

23 Bosely, Sarah, 'Kickbacks, cartels and chatrooms: how the unscrupulous drug firms woo the public', the *Guardian*, 26 June 2006

24 Law, Jacky, *Big Pharma*, Constable & Robinson, London, 2006, p.178

25 Herxheimer, Professor Andrew, 'Relationships between the pharmaceutical industry and patients' organisations', *British Medical Journal*, 2003, 326:1208–10

26 The *Sunday Times*, 15 October 2006

27 'Antidepressant drugs used as placebos', Alliance for Human Research Protection, 10 October 2003

ALLEN CARR'S EASYWAY CLINICS

The following pages list contact details for all Allen Carr's Easyway To Stop Smoking Clinics/Centres worldwide where the success rate, based on the three month money back guarantee, is over 90%.

Selected clinics also offer sessions that deal with alcohol and weight issues. Please check with your nearest clinic, which is listed, for details.

Allen Carr's Easyway guarantees that you will find it easy to stop smoking at the clinics or your money back.

Worldwide Head Office
Park House, 14 Pepys Road, Raynes Park, London SW20 8NH
Tel: +44 (0)208 944 7761 Email: mail@allencarr.com Website: www.allencarr.com
Worldwide Press Office
Tel: +44 (0)7970 88 44 52
Email:jd@statacom.net
UK Clinic Information and Central Booking Line 0800 389 2115 (Freephone)

UK CLINICS

London
Park House, 14 Pepys Road, Raynes Park, London SW20 8NH
Tel: 020 8944 7761
Fax: 020 8944 8619
Therapists: John Dicey, Sue Bolshaw, Sam Carroll, Colleen Dwyer, Crispin Hay, Jenny Rutherford, Emma Sole, Rob Fielding
Email: mail@allencarr.com
Website: www.allencarr.com

Aylesbury
Tel: 0800 0197 017
Therapists: Kim Bennett,
Emma Sole
Email: kim@
easywaybucks.co.uk
Website: www.allencarr.com

Belfast
Tel: 0845 094 3244
Therapist: Tara Evers-
Cheung
Email:
tara@easywayni.com
Website: www.allencarr.com

Birmingham
Tel & Fax: 0121 423
1227
Therapists: John Dicey,
Colleen Dwyer, Crispin
Hay, Rob Fielding
Email:
easywayadmin@tiscali.co.uk
Website: www.allencarr.com

Bournemouth
Tel: 0800 028 7257/
01425 272 757
Therapist: John Dicey,
Colleen Dwyer, Sam
Carroll, Emma Sole
Email:
easywayadmin@tiscali.co.uk
Website: www.allencarr.com

Brighton
Tel: 0800 028 7257
Therapists: John Dicey,
Colleen Dwyer, Sam
Carroll, Emma Sole
Email:
easywayadmin@tiscali.co.uk
Website: www.allencarr.com

Bristol
Tel: 0117 950 1441
Therapist: Charles
Holdsworth Hunt
Email: stopsmoking@
easywaybristol.co.uk
Website: www.allencarr.com

Cambridge
Tel: 0800 0197 017
Therapists: Kim Bennett,
Emma Sole
Email: kim@
easywaybucks.co.uk
Website: www.allencarr.com

Cardiff
Tel: 0117 950 1441
Therapist: Charles
Holdsworth Hunt
Email: stopsmoking@
easywaybristol.co.uk
Website: www.allencarr.com

Coventry
Tel: 0800 321 3007
Therapist: Rob Fielding
Email: info@
easywaycoventry.co.uk
Website: www.allencarr.com

Crewe
Tel: 01270 501 487
Therapist: Debbie
Brewer-West
Email: debbie@
easyway2stopsmoking.co.uk
Website: www.allencarr.com

Cumbria
Tel: 0800 077 6187
Therapist: Mark Keen
Email: mark@
easywaycumbria.co.uk
Website: www.allencarr.com

Derby
Tel: 0800 0197 017
Therapists: Kim Bennett,
Emma Sole
Email: kim@
easywaybucks.co.uk
Website: www.allencarr.com

Essex (opening 2008)
Tel: 0800 389 2115
Website: www.allencarr.com

Exeter
Tel: 0117 950 1441
Therapist: Charles
Holdsworth Hunt
Email: stopsmoking@
easywayexeter.co.uk
Website: www.allencarr.com

High Wycombe
Tel: 0800 0197 017
Therapists: Kim Bennett,
Emma Sole
Email: kim@
easywaybucks.co.uk
Website: www.allencarr.com

Ipswich (opening 2008)
Tel: 0800 389 2115
Website: www.allencarr.com

Kent
Tel: 0800 389 2115
Therapist: Angela
Jouanneau
Website: www.allencarr.com

Lancashire
Tel: 0800 077 6187
Therapist: Mark Keen
Email: mark@
easywaylancashire.co.uk
Website: www.allencarr.com

Leeds
Freephone: 0800 804 6796
Therapists: Rob Groves
Email: stopsmoking@
easywayyorkshire.co.uk
Website: www.allencarr.com

Leicester
Tel: 0800 321 3007
Therapist: Rob Fielding
Email: info@
easywayleicester.co.uk
Website: www.allencarr.com

Lincoln
Tel: 0800 321 3007
Therapist: Rob Fielding
Website: www.allencarr.com

Liverpool
Tel: 0800 077 6187
Therapist: Mark Keen
Email: mark@
easywayliverpool.co.uk
Website: www.allencarr.com

Manchester
Freephone: 0800 804 6796
Therapists: Rob Groves
Email: stopsmoking@
easywaymanchester.co.uk
Website: www.allencarr.com

Milton Keynes
Tel: 0800 0197 017
Therapists: Kim Bennett,
Emma Sole
Email: kim@
easywaybucks.co.uk
Website: www.allencarr.com

Newcastle/North East
Tel/Fax: 0191 581 0449
Therapist: Tony Attrill
Email:
info@stopsmoking-uk.net
Website: www.allencarr.com

Northampton
Tel: 0800 0197 017

Therapists: Kim Bennett,
Emma Sole
Email: kim@
easywaybucks.co.uk
Website: www.allencarr.com

Norwich (opening 2008)
Tel: 0800 389 2115
Website: www.allencarr.com

Nottingham
Tel: 0800 0197 017
Therapists: Kim Bennett,
Emma Sole
Email: kim@
easywaybucks.co.uk
Website: www.allencarr.com

Oxford
Tel: 0800 0197 017
Therapists: Kim Bennett,
Emma Sole
Email: kim@
easywaybucks.co.uk
Website: www.allencarr.com

Peterborough
Tel: 0800 0197 017
Therapists: Kim Bennett,
Emma Sole
Email: kim@

easywaybucks.co.uk
Website: www.allencarr.com

Portsmouth (opening
2008)
Tel: 0800 389 2115
Website: www.allencarr.com

Reading:
Tel: 0800 028 7257
Therapist: John Dicey,
Colleen Dwyer, Sam
Carroll, Emma Sole
Website: www.allencarr.com

Scotland
Sessions held throughout
Scotland
Tel: 0131 449 7858
Therapist: Joe Bergin
Email: info
@easywayscotland.co.uk
Website: www.allencarr.com

Sheffield
Freephone: 0800 804
6796
Therapist: Rob Groves
Email: stopsmoking@
easywayyorkshire.co.uk
Website: www.allencarr.com

Shrewsbury
Tel: 01270 501 487
Therapist: Debbie
Brewer-West
Email:
debbie@easyway2stopsmo
king.co.uk
Website: www.allencarr.com

Southampton
Tel: 0800 028 7257 /
01425 272 757
Therapists: John Dicey,
Colleen Dwyer, Sam
Carroll, Emma Sole
Email:
easywayadmin@tiscali.co.uk
Website: www.allencarr.com

Southport
Tel: 0800 077 6187
Therapist: Mark Keen
Email: mark@
easywaylancashire.co.uk
Website: www.allencarr.com

Staines/Heathrow
Tel: 0800 028 7257
Therapists: John Dicey,
Colleen Dwyer, Sam
Carroll, Emma Sole
Website: www.allencarr.com

Surrey
Park House, 14 Pepys
Road, Raynes Park,
London SW20 8NH
Tel: 020 8944 7761 Fax:
020 8944 8619
Therapists: John Dicey,
Sue Bolshaw, Sam
Carroll, Colleen Dwyer,
Crispin Hay, Jenny
Rutherford, Emma Sole,
Rob Fielding
Email: mail@allencarr.com
Website: www.allencarr.com

Stevenage
Tel: 0800 019 7017
Therapists: Kim Bennett,
Emma Sole
Email: kim@
easywaybucks.co.uk
Website: www.allencarr.com

Stoke
Tel: 01270 501 487
Therapist: Debbie
Brewer-West
Email:
debbie@easyway2stopsmo
king.co.uk
Website: www.allencarr.com

Swindon
Tel: 0117 950 1441
Therapist: Charles
Holdsworth Hunt
Email: stopsmoking@
easywaybristol.co.uk
Website: www.allencarr.com

Telford
Tel: 01270 501487
Therapist: Debbie
Brewer-West
Email:
debbie@easyway2stopsmo
king.co.uk
Website: www.allencarr.com

Watford (opening 2007)
Tel: 0800 389 2115
Website: www.allencarr.com

Worcester
Tel: 0800 321 3007
Therapist: Rob Fielding
Website: www.allencarr.com

WORLDWIDE CLINICS

REPUBLIC OF IRELAND
Dublin and Cork
Lo-Call (From ROI) 1
890 ESYWAY (37 99 29)
Tel: 01 499 9010 (4 lines)
Therapist: Brenda
Sweeney and Team
Email: info@allencarr.ie
Website: www.allencarr.com

AUSTRALIA
North Queensland
Tel: 1300 85 1175
Therapist: Tara Pickard-
Clark
Email:
nqld@allencarr.com.au
Website: www.allencarr.com
Sydney, New South Wales
Tel and Fax: 1300
785180
Therapist: Natalie Clays
Email:
nsw@allencarr.com.au
Website: www.allencarr.com

South Australia
Therapist: Phillip Collins
Tel: (08) 8341 0898 /
FREECALL: 1300 88 60
31
Email: sa@allencarr.com.au
Website: www.allencarr.com
South Queensland
Tel: 1300 855 806
Therapist: Jonathan Wills
Email: sqld@allencarr.com.au
Website: www.allencarr.com
Victoria, Tasmania, Act.
Tel: 03 9894 8866 or
1300 790 565 (Freecall)
Therapist: Gail Morris
Email:
info@allencarr.com.au
Website: www.allencarr.com
Western Australia
Therapist: Dianne Fisher
Tel: 1300 55 78 01
Email: wa@allencarr.com.au
Website: www.allencarr.com

AUSTRIA
Sessions held throughout
Austria. Free line tele-
phone for Information
and Booking:
0800RAUCHEN (0800

7282436)
Tel: 0043 (0)3512 44755
Therapist: Erich Keller-
mann and Team
Email: info@allen-carr.at
Website: www.allencarr.com

BELGIUM
Antwerp
Koningin Astridplein 27
B-9150 Bazel
Tel: 03 281 6255
Fax: 03 744 0608
Therapist: Dirk Nielandt
Email:
easyway@dirknielandt.be
Website: www.allencarr.com

BULGARIA
Therapist: Stoyan Tonev
Email: s.tonev@yahoo.com
Website: www.allencarr.com

CANADA
Toll free 1-866 666 4299
/905 8497736
Therapist: Damian O'Hara
Seminars held in Toronto
and Vancouver
Corporate programs avail-
able throughout Canada

Email: info@theeasyway
tostopsmoking.com
Website: www.allencarr.com

CHILE (opening 2008)
Therapist: Claudia
Sarmiento
Email: contacto@
allencarr.cl
Website: www.allencarr.com

**COLOMBIA, SOUTH
AMERICA**
Bogota
Tel: (571) 6271193
Therapists: Jose Manuel
Duran
Email: easywaycolombia@
cable.net.co
Website: www.allencarr.com

CYPRUS
Tel: 0035 77 77 78 30
Therapist: Kyriacos
Michaelides
Email:
info@allencarr.com.cy
Website: www.allencarr.com

CZECH REPUBLIC
Tel: 00420 774 568 748

or 00420 774 KOURIT
Therapist: Adriana
Dubecka
Email: terapeut@
allencarr.cz
Website: www.allencarr.com

DENMARK
Sessions held throughout
Denmark
Tel: 0045 70267711
Therapist: Mette Fonss
Email: mette@easyway.dk
Website: www.allencarr.com

ECUADOR
Tel & Fax: 02 2820 920
Therapist: Ingrid Wittich
Email: toisan@pi.pro.ec
Website: www.allencarr.com

FRANCE
Sessions held throughout
France. Central Booking
Line: 0800 FUMEUR
(Freephone)
Therapists: Erick Serre
and Team
Tel: 33 (4) 91 33 54 55
Email: info@allencarr.fr
Website: www.allencarr.com

GERMANY

Sessions held throughout
Germany
Free line telephone for
information and central
booking line:
08000RAUCHEN (0800
07282436)
Therapists: Erich Keller-
mann and Team
Tel: 0049 (0) 8031
90190-0
Email: info@allen-carr.de
Website: www.allencarr.com

GREECE

Sessions held throughout
Greece
Tel: 0030 210 5224087
Therapist: Panos Tzouras
Email: panos@allencarr.gr
Website: www.allencarr.com

ICELAND

Reykjavik
Tel: 553 9590
Therapist: Petur Einarsson
Email: easyway@easyway.is
Website: www.allencarr.com

INDIA (opening 2008)

Bangalore and Chennai
Therapist: Suresh Shottam
Website: www.allencarr.com

ISRAEL

Sessions held throughout
Israel
Tel: 03-5467771
Therapist/Trainer: Ramy
Romanovsky, Aviv
Leibovitz
Email: info@allencarr.co.il
Website: www.allencarr.com

ITALY

Sessions held throughout
Italy
Tel/Fax: 02 7060 2438
Therapist: Francesca
Cesati
Email: info@
easywayitalia.com
Website: www.allencarr.com

JAPAN

Sessions held throughout
Japan
Tel: 0081 3 3507 4020
Therapist: Miho Shimada
Email: info@allen-carr.jp
Website: www.allencarr.com

MAURITIUS
Tel: 00230 727 5103
Therapist: Heidi Houreau
Email: allencarrmauritius@
yahoo.com
Website: www.allencarr.com

MEXICO
Sessions held throughout
Mexico
Tel: 052 55 2623 0631
Therapist: Jorge Davo
and Mario Campuzano
Otero
Email: info@
allencarr-mexico.com
Website: www.allencarr.com

NETHERLANDS
Amsterdam
Tel: 020 465 4665 Fax:
020 465 6682
Therapist: Eveline de Mooij
Email: amsterdam@
allencarr.nl
Utrecht
Tel: 035 602 94 58
Therapist: Paula Rooduijn
Email: soest@allencarr.nl
Rotterdam
Tel: 010 244 0709 Fax:
010 244 07 10
Therapist: Kitty van't Hof

Email: rotterdam@
allencarr.nl
Nijmegen
Tel: 024 336 03305
Therapist: Jacqueline van
den Bosch
Email: nijmegen@
allencarr.nl
Website: www.allencarr.com

NEW ZEALAND
North Island -Auckland
Tel: 09 817 5396
Therapist: Vickie Macrae
E-mail: vickie@
easywaynz.co.nz
Website: www.allencarr.com
South Island –
Christchurch –
Opening 2008
Therapist: Laurence
Cooke
Website: www.allencarr.com

NORWAY
Oslo
Tel: 23 27 29 39
Therapist: Laila Thorsen
Email: post@
easyway-norge.no
Website: www.allencarr.com

POLAND
Sessions held throughout
Poland
Tel: 022 621 36 11
Therapist: Anna Kabat
E-Mail: info@allen-carr.pl
Website: www.allencarr.com

PORTUGAL
Oporto:
Tel: 22 9958698
Therapist: Ria Slof
Email: info@comod-
eixardefumar.com
Website: www.allencarr.com

SERBIA
Belgrade
Tel: (0)11 308 8686
Email:
office@allencarr.co.yu
Email: milos.rakovic@
allencarrserbia.com
Website: www.allencarr.com

SINGAPORE (opening
2008)
Therapist: Pam Oei
Website: www.allencarr.com

SLOVAKIA
Tel: 00421 908 572 551

Therapist: Adriana
Dubecka
Email: terapeut@
allencarr.sk
Website: www.allencarr.com

SOUTH AFRICA
Central Booking Line (in
SA): 0861 100 200
**Head office & Cape
Town clinic:**
15 Draper Square, Draper
St, Claremont 7708
Tel: 021 851 5883
Mobile: 083 600 5555
Therapist: Dr. Charles Nel
Email: easyway@
allencarr.co.za
Website: www.allencarr.com
Pretoria
Tel: 084 (EASYWAY) 327
9929
Therapist: Dudley Garner
Email:
info@allencarr.co.za
Website: www.allencarr.com

SPAIN
Sessions held throughout
Spain
Tel: 902 10 28 10 Fax:
942 83 25 84

Therapists: Geoffrey
Molloy & Rhea Sivi and
Team
E-mail: easyway@
comodejardefumar.com
Website: www.allencarr.com

SWEDEN
Goteborge & Malmö
Tel: 031 24 01 00
Email: info@allencarr.nu
Website: www.allencarr.com
Stockholm
Tel: 08 5999 5731
Therapist: Nina Ljingquist
Email: info@allencarr.se
Website: www.allencarr.com

SWITZERLAND
Sessions held throughout
Switzerland
Free line telephone for
Information and Booking:
0800RAUCHEN (0800
728 2436) Tel: 0041
(0)52 383 3773
Fax: 0041 (0)52
3833774
Therapist: Cyrill Argast
and Team
SESSIONS Suisse
Romand and Svizzera

Italia
Tel: 0800 386 387
Email: info@allen-carr.ch
Website: www.allencarr.com

TURKEY
Sessions held throughout
Turkey
Tel: 0090 212 358 5307
Trainer: Emre Ustunucar
email: info@
allencarrturkiye.com
Website: www.allencarr.com

USA
Sessions held throughout
the USA
Central information and
bookings: Toll Free:
1 866 666 4299
email: info@theeasyway
tostopsmoking.com
Website: www.allencarr.com
Seminars held regularly
in New York and
Los Angeles
Corporate programs avail-
able throughout the USA
Mailing address: 1133
Broadway, Suite 706,
New York. NY 10010
Therapist: Damian O'Hara